Indestructible You is a penetrating exploration into the source of the negative emotions that darken the human psyche. The book takes familiar terms from popular culture – "will," "power," "competition" – and using simple language reframes them into effective strategies for attaining authentic inner power. What's more, it does so in ways that resonate with, and even transcend some profound spiritual teachings. The lucid writing, personal examples and simple practical exercises shift readers from common attitudes of victimhood to becoming "heroes of their own lives." It is the sort of book which will be read and re-read as a practical manual of inspiration and empowerment.

Professor Louis G. Herman, Head of Political Science Department, University of Hawai'i West O'ahu and author of *Future Primal: How Our Wilderness Origins Show Us the Way Forward*

Shai Tubali has managed to develop a conclusive psychology of the will. His core thesis that "will precedes suffering" is a genuine key to increased autonomy. I have applied the ideas in *Indestructible You* in my own life and in my work with others, with astonishing results. His suggestion not to suppress and deny the will to power in certain areas of life, but to accept it and thus transform it complies with the most recent scientific research, which says that accepting an impulse, a thought or an emotion immediately "calms" it down. Struggling against it, on the other hand, creates stress and makes us sick and unhappy. After working with the exercises of this book I experienced an immediate physical relaxation and my clients have given me the same feedback. In sum, it's a very helpful book.

Inke Jochims, Psychotherapist, Hypnotherapist, NLP instructor and author of *Süchtig nach Süßem?*

Indestructible You is a welcome antidote for the pressures resulting from today's turbulent world and frantic lifestyles. Shai Tubali and Tim Ward write in a reader-friendly manner; the exercises they have created are practical, useful, and — for many readers — life-changing. This is a book that provides a road map for resilience, empowerment, and transformation.

Stanley Krippner, Ph.D., Alan Watts Professor of Psychology, Saybrook University and co-author of *Personal Mythology, Extraordinary Dreams and Haunted by Combat*

I loved *Indestructible You*, mainly because it is different: the approach, the psychological practices, the unique understanding of meditation. I believe that the journey the book offers would require courage. But readers who would say "yes" to it would truly grow and change. With challenging ideas and stimulating practices this beautiful book invites you to transform and apply your will to life. This invitation would allow you to live life to the fullest; it would allow you to build a self that can't be broken.

Dr. Itai Ivtzan, Senior Lecturer and Programme Leader, Masters in Applied Positive Psychology (MAPP), University of East London, and author of *Awareness Is Freedom: The Adventure of Psychology and Spirituality*

The great thing about this book is that it not only reveals the deepest drive behind everything we do in life. It also shows in a practical way how to turn this understanding into a reality of freedom and true power.

Theresa Bäuerlein, journalist and author of *Tussikratie* and *Das war der gute Teil des Tages*

Anyone interested in leadership development recognizes the importance of self-awareness. I found the combination of explanation, personal anecdote, and thought-provoking questions in

Indestructible You a delightful invitation to self-reflect. I must admit to becoming aware of some "habits of thinking" that I'd like to pay attention to as a result of having read this book.

Peter Schwartz, Best Practice Chair & Master Chair, Vistage International

An inspiring journey to the depths of the psyche.

Wade Davis, Professor of Anthropology, University of British Columbia, and author of *Into the Silence*

Indestructible You

Building a Self that Can't be Broken

Indestructible You

Building a Self that Can't be Broken

Shai Tubali & Tim Ward

CHANGE
MAKERS
BOOKS

Winchester, UK
Washington, USA

First published by Changemakers Books, 2015
Changemakers Books is an imprint of John Hunt Publishing Ltd., Laurel House, Station Approach,
Alresford, Hants, SO24 9JH, UK
office1@jhpbooks.net
www.johnhuntpublishing.com
www.changemakers-books.com

For distributor details and how to order please visit the 'Ordering' section on our website.

Text copyright: Shai Tubali and Tim Ward 2014

ISBN: 978 1 78279 940 5
Library of Congress Control Number: 2014958929

A CIP catalogue record for this book is available from the British Library.

Design: Stuart Davies

Printed in the USA by Edwards Brothers Malloy

We operate a distinctive and ethical publishing philosophy in all
areas of our business, from our global network of authors to
production and worldwide distribution.

CONTENTS

Chapter One

The life inside you

Find a moment in your life when you felt fully alive, energized and connected to everything around you. Perhaps you felt oneness with nature when you entered a rich green forest, or drew breath in the thin cold air on a mountaintop. Perhaps you raised your head in the dark desert and felt infinite galaxies streaming down upon you. You may have been surprised by spring flowers bursting with life and color, the birth of a baby, or an artist's canvas that overwhelmed you with beauty. Most likely you have experienced such a moment through life's most intense pleasures: sex, falling in love, having an adventure, or simply sharing a delicious meal with close friends.

For most people such moments are fleeting and all too rare. The purpose of this book is to share with you a way to deepen your sense of connection to life so that you can feel fully alive whenever you want. The method may surprise you. We want to strengthen your awareness of the most alive part in you, the driving life force at your core: your will.

Life is will. To be alive means to want, and to want means to be alive. Behind the seeming harmony of nature intense forces and urges are always at work. Not only the strongest and the fittest, but even the *nicest* living things intensely want. Songbirds sing to attract and impress mates and to proclaim territories; they sing loud and long to overcome the competing songs of other birds. It is not at all about singing hymns to God or expressing the harmonies of nature. The lovely spreading trees are really an evolutionary adaptation; by growing taller, trees are striving to outmaneuver each other to better reach the sunlight. The breathtaking colors of spring flowers are an intricate evolutionary scheme: they draw bees and other pollinators into service

1

of the plants' reproduction. When life creates beauty it is because it wants to reproduce. The act of procreation is simply the will to become more than what one already is. Life is never content with mere survival. Life forever wants to grow in power, to expand in numbers, to seize territories. For this reason, life rarely rests, and when it rests, it is to regain its power for this tireless activity.

The same is true for every person. To want is the most natural thing in life. To be human means to be driven by intense passions. Any birth of a child is the eruption of a willful creature, no matter how innocent and adorable that creature may appear. A toddler is never content with mere survival. A child wants to feel and touch, taste and experiment, grow and know, acquire and obtain. A child tirelessly seeks ways that could grant him or her a sense of fulfillment and realization, self-enhancement and self-expression. From birth onwards we humans are walking wills, wills with legs and hands and eyes. We are driven by the search for experiences of empowerment and growth, expansion and feelings of power. We are not different in this way than the rest of nature; we have only extended the will of life to new territories of feeling and thinking, relating and experiencing.

In life, no one just "wants to be." It is never enough just to be. This is the great difference between "being" and "becoming": to be means only to survive and breathe. Do you only want to breathe? Are you satisfied with your mere survival? Of course not. Even a plant stretches its leaves towards the sun and pushes its roots deeper into the soil. We, all of us, are in a feverish, incessant search for ways to grow, ways to fulfill and express ourselves more and more.

If you read this book, it means you want something. Most probably you want to gain more knowledge of yourself in order to become stronger, more present, more free and more in control. It is your will that has led you to read this book. If the book succeeds, and you start to feel your power grow, you will love it and read every page with excitement. If it fails, you will get rid of it, and search for something else. You like what makes you feel more powerful, more enhanced.

You can easily put this to the test right now with a brief thought experiment:

> Try just to be without any purpose whatsoever. Simply sit and be and breathe. How long do you think this can go on without the interruption of thoughts or feelings? Put the book down now, and experiment with this.

Our guess is that for most of you this experiment will end in the blink of an eye, and not because there's something wrong with you. The thoughts appear because there's too much excitement inside you; there is a constant bubbling of urges to become more, more than one presently is. At the root of all thoughts lies the very energy of wanting.

You can examine this by yourself. Thoughts are made of plans for the future (unfulfilled experiences that excite us) and regrets about the past (wanting to correct some experiences to get a better present and future). They are also made of fantasies (imagining what we really want to do yet cannot do in reality) and efforts to control life through internal arguments with reality (our wishes to overpower life in order to get what we want). Of course that's not a complete list of all our thoughts. But if you looked deeply into any thought, you would find that they all boil down to one inner force: wishes to gain some sort of power in the real world.

Some might say: "But what about negative feelings and thoughts? They don't seem to want. In fact they come over us as a depressed letting go of all wanting." We will explore why this is so later on. For now, to demonstrate how negative thoughts and feelings are also wanting, please think of one of your own negative thoughts that has plagued you. Turn that thought over like a rock. You will see on its underside that your thought is just a frustration – a frustration of will.

Now try just sitting and being again. Try sincerely to just be and to remain content with mere being. This time, as the thoughts and feelings bubble up, see if you can notice something that feels like a frantic search going on inside of you. We want so badly to get up and move around, to experience and get involved in the stream of life. If we force ourselves to sit motionless, our thoughts start doing it for us: they move around and get involved. Indeed, it is terribly difficult to sit quietly, both externally and internally, for too long.

Sometimes, when we become exhausted from this race of will, we desperately *want* to relax. To relax means not to want anything in particular for a certain period of time. But even while relaxing, we often yearn for some experience of pleasure that would enhance us and enrich our senses: good food, good sex, happy feelings, exciting adventures. Relaxation also serves our will. It is for the renewal of our energy. In other words, we relax only to acquire the sufficient energy to get back to the search for self-fulfillment.

Different schools of meditation have encouraged many millions in the Western world to aspire to this state of just being without wanting. From the point of view of such schools, to ceaselessly want is to be trapped in a state of suffering. Wanting, they say, is a state of restlessness which should be considered an existential neurosis that all humans share. The Buddha (and many gurus after him) taught that the state of human suffering could be ended by ceasing to desire – a process which required rigorous training through many lifetimes. Respectfully, we disagree.

The problem is that meditation, if understood as the complete quietude of the mind, is an unnatural state, while this restlessness is a natural state. We are like a flame of life that cannot extinguish itself. We are too excited because life's excitement is what we are. Stopping our restlessness temporarily through meditation can help us smooth out the rough edges of our frenzied search for power. It can recharge our batteries. But negating suffering can't be your life's purpose.

Seeking quietude as an end in itself sets you up to resist life's dynamic energy. It's as if you are stuck on a roller coaster and all you are doing is trying to get off the ride. So you close your eyes and pretend you are not moving. We believe it's better to keep your eyes wide open and do something constructive with the inescapable energy of life. The paradoxical situation of the genuinely devoted meditator is that he or she in practice is a very willful person: the path to meditative quietness requires a tremendous amount of desire, and a strong enough will to gather one's entire concentration and energy, intention and ambition in order to achieve this goal of tranquility. Ironically, the great teachers of this path can be found ceaselessly lecturing, teaching, and energetically training disciples to spread their methods for "letting go."

The simple truth is that we cannot stop wanting. Wanting is the tireless engine of life itself. Even the act of breathing is not a letting go; it is a grasping for life. Have you ever struggled for your breath underwater or during an asthma attack? You want your breath with all the will in you.

We may not like it, how much we want. We may fear that if we feel the full force of our desire it will be bad for us. Resistance to the idea of wanting as the core of our being is fueled by two major reasons: the first one is morality, and the second is our past emotional injuries.

Morality, as we have acquired it since early childhood, encourages us to adopt a self-image that we are good, loving, selfless, and moral. This self-image helps us to hide away our endless wanting; hide it away even from ourselves. Morality is like the famous fig leaves that Adam and Eve used to cover their genitals after they first sinned. But what morality really covers up is will, which is our true nature. It covers it up so well that our true nature never enters our self-image. If someone would come and say to you: "You are a walking will, a seething cauldron of desire," you would most probably be offended!

It is not considered "good" to be willful. The "good" person doesn't want, at least not too much. It is good to be satisfied with very little. Only the bad ones want without shame. The good, like us, live humbly with what they have already got and very gently wish for some improvement of our lot sometime in the future, or perhaps a reward in heaven. When we want, we make sure that it appears as almost not-wanting; as just getting a little something for ourselves in the world which belongs to the "powerful."

The other reason one might resist the world of will is our past injuries and wounds. These wounds, inflicted by experiences of weakening and deep frustration, have taught us that wanting too much usually leads to painful disappointment. We learned early on that life and people can dramatically rob us of any sense of power and will and leave us feeling vulnerable and helplessly small. In fact, if you look deeply into your most difficult and humiliating experiences, you will find out that they always had something to do with the loss of your power. As walking wills, it is intolerable for us to remain so utterly powerless, with our wills and wishes defeated.

The experience of weakening happens when our feeling of power dramatically diminishes. We can reach a minimal state in which our wills are shattered, often due to the overpowering of stronger forces with a greater will: abused by a parent, bullied in school, fired from a job, rejected by a lover. Such experiences make us seek alternative, internal and secret solutions that alleviate and compensate for our position of weakness. They make us quietly retreat from the game of life, be cautious with our wanting, and careful not to reveal our true desires. The experience of weakening makes us turn our heads away from the will that burns at the core of our being, and focus instead on the "miserable we," the forlorn victims of life.

Since we often don't deal properly with our experiences of weakening, they gradually erode our connection to life as will. Add to that the moral self-image, and you'll grasp why we cannot get in touch with our true nature. This book will guide you back to it, to who you really are. The first step is for you to acknowledge the will to grow and expand as your life's driving force.

It is amazing how merely acknowledging this driving force can strengthen you at once. It's like getting you on your feet, as your real self, connected to the flame of life at the core of your being. This self-recognition is a key to unlocking a constant inner state of power, a power that cannot diminish. This is what we call *True Inner Power*. On your way towards this inner power, identifying yourself as a continuum of will serves as a highly effective way to master your mental and emotional distresses. All your memories of weakening, and all your present experiences of weakening, can be dealt with differently if you begin by affirming your life's basic wish for power.

In reality, we are already connected to a tremendous power: the *biological* power of life and the *physical* power of the cosmos. Each one of us embodies this power. This is not a metaphor. Every particle in your being came from the Big Bang. That explosion of energy, that drive to expand, still throbs in us. It is us. We are the ripples of the Big Bang in human form. We can realize that right away if we only acknowledge the pounding will that drove us to become alive in the first place. Close your eyes for a second: can you feel that pulse of life within you, that electricity, that "thing" that *wants to be alive*?

Our ability to feel that "thing" is only hindered by moral limitations and wounded memories. Both restrain and blur this innate, natural power. A power that is yours, because it is you.

Connecting with this power can be exhilarating, and it is important to realize at the start that unleashing your inner power is something fundamentally different than a toddler's furious demand that the world give her everything she wants. This is not a book about the immediate satisfaction of your every desire. It's more akin to the guiding theme of the *Spiderman* movies: "With great power comes great responsibility." This book will guide you how to initiate a conscious communication with this great natural power inside you, stop denying it and start using it to better cope with the phenomenon of life. You only need true knowledge of the real life, your life and the life of the cosmos, and that knowledge will powerfully reshape the reality of your psyche.

It might sound strange, but this is not just a book for reading. It is also a tool for thinking clearly and feeling deeply. To this end, you will find exercises and thought experiments in text boxes within each chapter. Please stop reading and do them as you come across them. You will also find practices for you to do after you have read each chapter. These are valuable tools to enable you to test out and integrate these new ideas into your daily life.

Shai Tubali
Tim Ward

Chapter Two

The root of all negative emotions

"Really, I'm a walking will?" you might respond to Chapter One. "But I only *occasionally* feel that I really want something, and even when I do, I often don't express it, let alone act aggressively to get what I want."

So in Chapter Two let's look for convincing evidence for your will. We will find it where you might least expect: in your negative emotions. In Chapter One we said your negative emotions were like a rock, and if you turned it over and looked beneath, you would find your will hidden there. Your negative emotions are the reflectors of your inner reality. They arise from the frustration of your will. As long as your life is going along smoothly, things are working out as you desire, and you are getting what you want, you don't notice your will. It's when you encounter an obstacle and your will is blocked that it reveals itself. Think of your negative emotions as like branches on a tree. Frustration forms the trunk of that tree – the common factor that upholds all these negative feelings. And the roots that nourish and support trunk and branches are your willful being.

You can follow a very simple and powerful method for discovering for yourself how frustrated will lies behind every negative emotion:

Think of a recent time when you felt a powerful negative emotion. What exactly frustrated you in that situation? Can you identify a will behind that frustration? Let's say, for example, that you felt insulted by something that a close friend said to you. What will hides behind this

---

insult? Most likely you want this friend's appreciation. Perhaps this friend appreciates you for the most part, but you want more. You want that friend to appreciate you *all the time*, to respect and encourage you without reservation. If you look even more deeply – perhaps you wanted the appreciation of *everyone* around you all the time. When this friend hurt and disregarded you, you might have felt that your status was undermined: that you were moving to that unpleasant side of life, the side of the weak. You wanted that feeling of power gained by others' appreciation to stay. Your insult, then, was the outcome of your will, and it was this will, this expectation, that was threatened and hurt, not anything else inside you.

The next step in proving to yourself that your will lies behind your negative emotions is to keep a diary for a certain period – for a month, a week, a few days or even only for a single day. Whenever you experience some negative emotion, whether it is frustration, disappointment, jealousy or sadness, write it down. Then be with it for a moment and ask yourself: what is it that I wanted to get and didn't get? What will of mine was thwarted here? Sometimes, especially in certain fears and anxieties, you will need to rephrase the question: what is it that I want to achieve or hold on to that might be thwarted in that scary future image?

In the case of being insulted by your friend, you might write in your diary:

Insulted by an unsupportive friend. – Expecting and wanting to get the others' appreciation all the time.

I (Shai) would like to share an example of what happened when some of my clients realized that will lay behind their negative emotions. Recently I guided a sixty-year-old optometrist through this process of discovering his will. He was a generous, gentle, sensitive and cheerful man, a professional admired by the customers of his small store in the mall. Yet whenever someone complained about the quality of the glasses they bought from him or the service they received, he would get such attacks of rage that he had to turn the customer over to his wife, who works with him. He would whisper to her as he headed for the back room, "You take care of this guy, otherwise I might kill him!" Looking at this friendly and sensitive man, I wondered how he could possibly want to murder his customers. I asked what he thought was the cause of his rage. He told me that a psychologist who treated him diagnosed a deep-seated sense of helplessness. I encouraged him to explore what will lay behind his feeling of helplessness. At one point the optometrist started laughing: "It is because I want all of them to be one hundred percent of the time appreciative and admiring. I want everyone to admire me. That's my expectation! And I won't accept less than one hundred percent; even ninety-nine percent admiration is not enough!" He laughed because he realized that he wanted to be king of his store, which isn't very realistic when you're serving customers rather than commanding fearful subjects of one's realm.

Another person who came to me (Shai) recently was a frail young man who had suffered for years from extreme and debilitating anxiety. He was an inward-looking type: deeply immersed in his inner world, brooding all day long. He seemed to be caught in a self-perpetuating cycle of fear. He wrote to me enthusiastically after a few months of following this practice of uncovering the will behind negative emotions: "I'm really starting to get that it is my will *to become a somebody* that is the source of all my emotional distress. People bring themselves to states of severe crises, even become suicidal, only because they cannot accept the fact that things did not happen as they wanted them to happen. And then comes the greatest illusion: my will did not come true, therefore I'm a victim!" The young man's note to me concluded: "I understand now that there is no such thing as a *fear of losing control*. My only fear is that my will won't be fulfilled."

If you seriously and honestly explore all your negative emotions with this practice, in a very short while you will realize negative emotions are actually your wills in disguise. Even when you feel horribly victimized or depressed to death, dig beneath the feeling and you will uncover a will. This is the key to freeing yourself from the grip of these seemingly overwhelming feelings.

This is the simple principle you will discover: *feeling follows willing*. First there is a will. Only afterwards comes the negative emotion.

You might ask, "Then, why isn't this obvious? Why don't we perceive the inner workings of our mind in this order? Why do we sense the feeling first, and then have to dig for the willing?" The short answer is: your self-image works to protect you from recognizing your will. Remember in Chapter One we described self-image as a mechanism that helps us hide away our endless wanting behind a picture of our self as a good, loving, unselfish and moral person? When your will is thwarted, the self-image diverts your attention away from the will and towards the negative emotion to keep you from confronting the fact that you are at heart a willing being, rather than a good person. But the unfortunate by-product of this protective maneuver is that it makes you think you are the helpless *victim* of your suffering, rather than the *cause* of your suffering.

Suffering is simply the feeling that spreads inside you when you don't get what you want: when life denies you what you expect. It always seems unfair to find yourself on the losing side of life, because for some reason, you always assume that your wills are unlike any other wills in this universe. Your wills are the right wills, the things that *surely* must happen in real life.

Here the truth of negative emotions is clearly revealed: they are your tireless battle with the world, the constant clash between your wills and "real life." As long as everything is "fine" – that is, the world pretty much matches your will – you are pleased and more or less peaceful. This is why it seems to you during the "pleasing" times that you are not driven by intense wills at all. But when there's a clash, and the fulfillment of your will is denied by reality, you respond with resistance and hostility and show your "true face." This is where the different negative emotions arise, and where you begin to suffer.

We can now refine our principle that *feeling follows willing*. We can say: suffering happens when bad feelings follow thwarted willing. Or more simply, *Will precedes suffering*.

Religions and various spiritual and philosophical schools of thought attempted to come to terms with this law by trying to annihilate all wills in order to reach some minimal state of existence, so minimal that it would almost be like nonexisting. For example, the Buddhist term *nirvana* literally means "to extinguish." To go back to our tree metaphor, these schools aimed to get rid of the branches of bad feelings by chopping off the roots of the will. In this way, so they hoped, they would liberate themselves forever from pain and suffering. This is not our solution. We don't believe one can stop being a walking will, since life is will. If you really chopped off the roots, you would be effectively dead. For this reason, this new awareness we want to awaken in you is not to help you put an end to your will. It is only meant to show you how you can better work with the will that is your authentic inner truth and use it to expand your genuine inner power.

Tracing your suffering to its roots in your hidden will gives you self-knowledge. But this is just the first stage of the practice. The second stage gives you the power to change your life. Once you grasp that your suffering is the frustration of your will, you are able to take responsibility for it. Yes, *you* are the cause of your suffering. That means you, and you alone, have the power to change it.

We already said that there is nothing more natural than wanting, yet everything comes at a price. When you want, your will is sometimes overpowered by others' will. You are not the only player in this game. The world is full of people, full of wills. Expecting to have the upper hand over all other people, all the time is childish. It's what a two-year-old wants. That is why the second stage of the practice is a radical act of maturity. Having revealed your will and acknowledged it clearly, you will need to ask yourself: is this will worth fighting for and suffering for? There are three ways to go from here:

1. *Keep it.* Is this will of yours worth fighting for? Great. Just don't complain if your struggle for what you want entails suffering. If in its present form this will doesn't match reality's stronger stream, accept that it will cost you some pain and tremendous effort if you choose to persevere.
2. *Replace it.* Consciously replace the will you have with a more harmonious route of self-expansion. Think for a moment: is there some way to fulfill your will in a different form?
3. *Release it.* Realize that your will in this instance is simply childish and unrealistic. In that case, just let it go and move on with your life. This will cut off the roots of the negative emotions that nourished and sustained the negative emotions.

There are many unrealistic expectations inside us. Some of them are pretty funny when you see them through the perspective of the will. Two examples:

"I'm really angry with this traffic jam," reveals the expectation: "I don't mind traffic jams generally speaking, but when I'm around, I expect the roads to be always clear and free."

"I'm exhausted from my tight schedule and overwork," reveals the expectation: "I want to have it all: to get all my ambitions fulfilled, to enjoy social communication, to engage in romantic relationship, to be a good father or mother, to be rich and successful, and even relaxed and peaceful – all at the same time!"

Whether you choose to keep the will, replace it or release it, the crucial act here is to take full responsibility for your choice. You cannot allow yourself to put on that miserable face of the wretched victim (well, unless you *want* to and then *choose* to!). If you deeply take in this practice, you will find that you are able to cut out the emotional drama in your life, stop playing the victim and turn your attention to the true creator of your feelings: *you*.

This simple practice has changed the life of many. It has also changed my own life (Shai). Lecturing in front of large and small audiences has been part of my work for many years. Over time I developed some elegant solutions that made the experience more comfortable and relaxing for me. But I could never deal well with seeing a dissatisfied listener. An irritated face or a bored expression would make me feel terribly uncomfortable and distracted. Even in a crowded room of happy listeners, my entire attention would turn to that one dissatisfied face. I used to regard it as some form of "hypersensitivity" and my friends and supporters lovingly encouraged me to keep thinking like that. However, that excuse was completely overturned when I started developing the principle of *Will precedes suffering*.

I could see that there was nothing "hypersensitive" about me. On the contrary, I was so domineering, so utterly controlling, that I wanted all my audience, without exception, to submit to my perfect lecture. My lectures were like a form of art that no one would be allowed to disrupt, so my hearers were just silent and inactive participants in my own play. I wasn't sensitive. I was more like a violent and crazy tyrant who couldn't tolerate even the slightest opposition. As soon as I realized this, I was no longer "sensitive" during my lectures and could let anyone, including myself, breathe and relax.

When you want to go on stage, you cannot complain that sometimes your audience doesn't like you. Your desire attracts new situations, which are by nature more risky. Wanting to be powerful or influential or admired can cost you humiliation and weakening as well. But we tend to forget that these situations were shaped by our desire for power and self-expansion. We shift our attention to the pain and insult, and usually get our friends' and family's attention and pity. If you have a friend who listens carefully to your tearful complaint, and then says: "But how can you complain? You have brought that on yourself. Remember, you wanted to be famous! Grow up and take responsibility for your own desires!" – consider yourself lucky. If you don't push that friend aside and start looking for the more empathic friends, if you manage to resist the temptation of self-pity and instead dust yourself off and get back on your feet, that means you're already intuitively getting the second stage of the practice.

I (Tim) vividly recall a time in my life when I chose to replace a will that was making me suffer with a different will. In my early thirties I had my first literary travel book published with great reviews in Canada, and I realized what I wanted in life was to be a full-time author and travel writer. Though I lived quite simply, after two years of poverty and a child to support, I faced the unpleasant prospect of needing a "real" job. I felt deeply frustrated. I wanted to be the special sort of person whose artistic talent alone could support him. Why wouldn't publishers recognize my awesomeness and offer me a big advance? At that time, my father invited me to join him in his line of work – communications training. He said to me, "This work pays well, so you could do it part time, and still devote yourself to your writing, without worrying about paying your bills." It was wrenching to compromise my dream. But I realized the reason I wanted to live off my writing was to gain freedom. It turned out the communications work was just as creative and satisfying. It has taken care of all my financial needs and still has left the time to write several more books. Replacing my frustrated will with a more realistic one gave me the freedom I desired, and actually opened up the path to more travel as my teaching took me around the world.

All negative states of the psyche boil down to this single principle of *will precedes suffering*. This is easiest to detect when it comes to anger. Put simply, anger is one's anxious attempt to force reality to accept one's will. Yet anger often hides behind a sense of victimhood. In weaker emotions, such as fear, anxiety, or depression, it can take practice to locate the will.

Fear is the will's little baby. It arises with the possibility you will lose what you desire. No desire, no fear. So a fearful person is actually a will-full person. Fear arises when you feel powerless to struggle for what you want in a specific circumstance. You know that there are stronger forces at play that you can't control, and that you are not equipped well enough to withstand the challenge. For example:

"I'm afraid I will fail in the exam." – I want so much to succeed. I'm only uncertain that I have what it takes to make it, so I'm in a minimal degree of control.

Anxieties are a compulsive wish for a tremendous power over all the possible routes that life might take. You are anxious because you seek full control of everything in order to prevent any dissatisfying outcome. You wish for godlike powers that would allow you to hold the reins of fate in your own hands. For example:

"I am always anxious that one of my relatives might die." – I want all my relatives to somehow exist out of death's reach.

Frankly, I want all of us to be safe forever from any possible harm!

Depression is our unending childish sorrow over a certain loss of power (or the inability to attain some hoped-for power). You may feel inept in this particular power struggle, perhaps even in the general power struggle of life, and so you withdraw from the play altogether. There is often a silent defiance in depression: "I'm not playing anymore! This game is no longer my concern!" Still, here too you could reverse the feeling:

"I am depressed." – I want life to give me what I want, without my effort. I want life to take care of me because I don't feel strong enough to get what I want through my own resources.

It's not actually the negative emotions that need your careful diagnosis and care. As with any disease, it's not wise to treat only the symptoms. If you're struggling to find your way out of depression, you are actually trapped in the symptom rather than looking into the source of your dis-ease.

Whenever you suffer from some emotional weakness, strive to locate the forcefulness of your will beneath it. It is the forcefulness that causes the weakness. *As soon as you deal with the forcefulness, the weakness will miraculously dissolve.* We know it may sound incredible that fear, anxiety, even depression can simply dissolve. But it's real and even simpler than it sounds in written words. It's actually easier to dissolve weakness in this manner than it is to try and free yourself from negative emotions by fixating on them, as happens in some forms of therapy. Since fear, anxiety and depression are all false states (illusions that are no more than psychological manipulations) no amount of understanding or rationalizing them will make them go away. That merely makes the illusions seem more real, as we will explain in later chapters. Working directly with your will is efficient. It only requires honesty. As soon as you find such honesty within yourself, you will discover your negative emotions naturally fall away.

Now that you have read this chapter, will you find yourself saying...

"I'm so frustrated right now. I wonder, what will of mine is being blocked? If I can find it, I can figure out if I want to keep it, replace it or release it."

"I'm so *angry* at her. But what is my anger telling me that I really want in this situation?"

"I feel depressed. I guess that means I'm not satisfied just sitting around moping. *Will precedes suffering* – so what desire wants to come alive in me? If I take responsibility for my will, I know I can reconnect with my power and let the feelings of helplessness dissolve."

Chapter Three

Napoleon and you

In the last chapter we said that the key to unleashing the energy of your inner power was in uncovering the forcefulness of your will. In this chapter we are going to explore how that forcefulness appears in your life. Then in the chapters to follow, we will look for the ways in which that forcefulness of will gets sidetracked and dissipated. This will then set you on the journey to recovering your power.

Your will takes shape in your mind as a wish. That wish creates an expectation, an expectation that life will fall into place around your wish as if by magic. For example, imagine yourself driving to your doctor's office for your annual checkup at 10am. You left home with plenty of time, but there's a traffic jam. You are stuck. The minutes tick by. You are going to be late. What are you feeling? Frustration. Anger at the other drivers for being in your way. It never occurs to you that in each car is another person stuck, late and just as frustrated as you. They are all reduced to obstacles in your world of one.

Finally traffic is moving again and though you get to the office late, you discover the doctor is not ready to see you yet. For an hour you sit, steaming. Your day is in ruins. Meetings will be missed. You hate this doctor and her staff who obviously have no idea how to run an office. It doesn't occur to you that other patients are the reasons for the delay, each with medical needs, some of them perhaps more urgent and complicated than your own. At that moment, in your mind the doctor exists only to serve you. So it goes throughout the day until you return home at last to your beloved partner. You yearn for soft words of comfort from this special person's lips and a warm hug, because that will make you feel better. Instead your partner acts cold towards you, barely feigns interest in your awful day but only wants to talk about some trivial annoyance that happened in *their* life. Now the two of you are arguing and next thing you know you are screaming like a child, "What about my needs?! Why are you never there for *me?*"

This is the frustrated scream of the primordial wish. A wish that wants *my will* at the center of the universe. It's a wish each of us carried from the moment we were born and cried out to be fed, to be held, to have our soiled diapers changed. If you are a parent, or were old enough to remember a sibling's early childhood, then you doubtless remember the "terrible twos." When a toddler's will is thwarted, this adorable little person transforms into a defiant and wild hell-spawn. They will kick, bite, hit, and throw themselves on the floor as if demon-possessed. They want what they want, and act as if they will die if they don't get it. If you know a young child going through this phase, go and watch them for a while. When a tantrum strikes, don't try and stop it. Just watch it unfold in wonder, as if witnessing a destructive tornado or a lightning storm. This is nature's raw fury, freely expressed in human form. Imagine what it would be like if you could harness and direct all of that energy and forcefulness.

The truth is, we are not much different than a toddler. We have this tremendous power at our disposal, but because we throw up a fantasy (our expectation that the entire world will bend to our wish) the power gets dissipated through our negative emotions, rather than directed to flow freely with purpose and intelligence. How did we end up this way?

To start with, as nature's children, we are biologically programmed to grow and thrive. Each of us arrived in the world with this will and this wish deeply embedded in our being. When we first encountered this world, we experienced it as ours to conquer. We could draw into ourselves milk, warmth and comfort, and make bad sensations and smells go away by our screaming. Our first expectation was that life should be pleasant always and conform to our desires without friction. You perhaps carried a residue of this expectation of omnipotence into early childhood. Perhaps you even imagined you possessed great powers and could manipulate reality. When I (Shai) was seven, I believed that I could control the changing of traffic lights with my mind. It took some time until I became convinced by clear evidence that that wasn't really so. And I (Tim) remember being enthralled by comic book superheroes, imagining that someday soon I was going to develop superpowers of my own. All I needed was a radioactive spider to bite me...

Your primordial wish came ready to rule the world. But this life comes with its own terms. They are unwritten and undeclared. No one asked you to sign the contract. It was signed without your permission at the moment of your birth. In reality, the life you were born into is almost completely out of your control. Blasted by events and people during your childhood, you, like each of us, were forced to realize that this life was not really *yours* to control. It would not attend to your screaming. As you grew, you entered larger and larger circles of life: your immediate family to your neighborhood and friends, your school, your community. At each step, life seemed more and more indifferent to your wishes. What was once a seamlessly whole life began to appear to you as an external world, a place separate from you that did not care about your wishes. Imagine how intolerable this must have been, this splitting of your life into two parts: your tiny being, and everything else. To survive you made a compromise, as each one of us have done. You began to create an inner world, a world that was much easier on you because your primordial wish was always at the center of it. This inner world started as a comforting fantasy land of your imagination. Gradually it became your world of thought: a safe place where you could escape the indifferent external world, and where your primal wish could rule.

Of course you don't think you dwell in two worlds, do you? You think you dwell in one world. But you mistake your inner fantasy world for the real one. You don't actually know the external world at all. We are sure this sounds outrageous to you. How could you test this for yourself? There is a simple way. Does your primordial wish lie at the center of the real, objective world? No, of course not. Is your primordial wish at the center of the world of your daily reality? Let's see. Mentally go back to the trip to the doctor's office. When you get frustrated, angry and upset, what comes to the surface? Your primal will, your inner toddler screaming, "What about *my* needs?"

This is why you fight the world all day long. You fight because you believe your primordial wish dwells at the heart of the world. Deep inside, you know this is a fantasy, but most likely you feel that if you gave up the fight, life would defeat you. Robbed of your remaining pride and will, what would be the point of living?

To survive, you make a second compromise. You split yourself into two persons. First, there's the "you" who is the unashamed will, who wants to get the world by the tail and make it bow down to all your wishes. Second, there is "you" who is the socially acceptable, fully-under-control persona who follows the rules. The second "you" is usually the stronger, since it gets all the support from society. Society, of course, is a collection of individual wills that as a combined force seems to have a will of its own. Much of society's will is dedicated to suppressing the wills of individuals for the supposed good of the group. So this second "you" takes its cues from society and represses the first "you," the willful "you." The social "you" hides the willful "you" away, but it doesn't really know what to do with it. It's like having something in your house you don't want people to see but you can't bear to throw away. So you put it into a box and then stash it in the basement. You hope it will be forgotten with time. In this way the primordial wish has remained intact inside you. You live and act as two persons: the hidden struggling will and the submissive citizen.

This is the reason for your daily struggles: you walk in the world like a toddler in an adult body, helplessly trying to make things happen to fulfill your will. Though you keep colliding with reality, you refuse to accept that your will is just one among billions of wills, and that as far as the external world is concerned, it is not important at all. So you cling to the hallucination of a parallel reality in which you can freely shape events and people. You devote massive amounts of energy to proving you are right, that you can bend others to your will. You cling to the fantasy so hard, you can't tell the difference between it and reality until reality breaks through and leaves you thwarted and frustrated. At that point the willful "you" pops like a jack-in-the-box out of the box in the basement, screaming, "What about my needs?"

Your fate is like that of a banished dictator – like Napoleon on the Isle of Corsica. You are at heart a megalomaniac world-ruler who doesn't understand why the world fails to listen to his perfect vision. The Napoleon in you declares without shame: "I will be fully content and relaxed only if life will submit to my authority." Everything would be wonderful for the whole world, if only everyone obeyed! Accustomed to commanding armies that conquer in his name, in captivity this Napoleon is forced to constrain his aggression, which turns into tension like a clenched fist. Your daily tension, the tension you feel in the car, the office, at home.

Real autocrats like Hitler and Stalin actually serve as good reminders of what can happen when individuals get to fulfill their primordial wish without compromise. You might think you would be a benign dictator. Is that really so? You will find your inner dictator in your bursts of aggression, where you lose control, rage, demand and threaten, perhaps even harm. You can also glimpse this inner tyrant when you judge everyone and everything, as if you were some god who knows what is absolutely right and what is absolutely wrong. Whenever I (Tim) find myself expressing uncompromising expectations that others will do as I think best, my wife says to me something like, "So, when you're the ruler of the world will we *all* have to do it your way?" That literally breaks the tension, and I can laugh.

Here's a short list of universal rules our inner dictators would dearly love to impose:

Everyone should adore me *unconditionally at all times,* no matter what I do, no matter how terrible or hostile I am.

I must *always* enjoy life *without interruption.*

I want to receive her/his love *forever* and know it could *never* go away.

I am *right about everything* all the time, and anyone who disagrees with me is an idiot.

I shall forever be the *fairest/smartest/strongest of them all!*

The primordial wish wants all your wills to be fulfilled without the slightest compromise. You want to *never* be on the weak side of life and to *always* have the upper hand. Or you want to be *completely* your "true self" and to never compromise your "true voice" – as if the most powerful people, from Barack Obama to Justin Bieber to the Queen of England, can freely be their "true self"! Or perhaps you believe that you, of all people, are destined for greatness. Some advertisers and popular speakers manip-ulate this desire when they promise you that *everything* is possible if you only "believe" in yourself and that *everyone* can become geniuses, powerful or simply have the life they always dreamed of. There is an entire industry built around the book *The Secret* and its well-known "Law of Attraction." According to this law, if you want something hard enough, you will draw it to yourself. Here's a brief description of the book from

Amazon.com:

> The Secret *contains wisdom from modern-day teachers – men and women who have used it to achieve health, wealth, and happiness. By applying the knowledge of* The Secret, *they bring to light compelling stories of eradicating disease, acquiring massive wealth, overcoming obstacles, and achieving what many would regard as impossible.*

One part of you leaps out and wants this, even as another part of you knows it can't possibly be true. You can identify these two parts now – your willful self with its primordial wish, and your compromising social self.

We won't make magical promises like *The Secret*. Instead what we can offer is a way to reconnect with the power of your primordial wish in such a way that you can make better use of it in the real world you share with eight billion others. To do this, we would first ask you to remove your primordial wish from the box in your mental basement, not out of frustration and negative emotions – the way it usually emerges – but calmly, deliberately, so you can better understand what exactly is at your core. Each person's primordial wish is somewhat different, with its own desires, even sometimes conflicting ones. To bring your deepest wishes out in the open, let's use a traditional route: the genie in the lamp.

Imagine you've got the shining ancient lamp in your hands right now. You rub it. The genie appears. Have fun with this exercise. Imagine it vividly, as if it is really happening. What will you ask for?

Your wish is my command…

Did you immediately feel you brushed up against an intense cultural taboo? Although everyone wishes for endless power, no one is allowed to admit it. You will have to shake off this resistance and the fear that you will be judged if you confess what you honestly want. This wish has been so severely thwarted in your lifetime it is deeply buried beneath negative emotions. Uncovering your primordial wish means setting your will free and *daring to want*. When you dare to want, you become a full and energetic participant in life. This is not at all the same as having your wish magically come true. Instead, it is about identifying the specific nature of your own primordial wish so that you can use that energy in the real world. It's not about getting everything you want, but about gaining a better flow of the life force within you. Now try the exercise again. This time throw yourself wholeheartedly into it.

Your wish is my command…
Listen to yourself as you accept this invitation. You don't have to choose just yet. Ponder your options. Feel free to choose more than one wish. You have three wishes, right? You can even break the standard genie rule and wish for more wishes if you want. If nothing comes to you at once, think about the things that frustrate you most in life, as we did in Chapter Two. Turn them over and see what will lies underneath. Imagine that wish being granted and the frustration immediately disappearing.

Write down what comes to you. Express it, loud and clear. There's great energy hidden here so don't be shy. Your self-image of "goodness" might tell you that it's terrible to do so, like that little angel sitting on a cartoon character's shoulder whispering not to give in to temptation. Brush it off your shoulder. You are not going to do anything rash. You are not going to act on these revealed wishes (your social self is still in control). You are simply recognizing a truth about yourself: a truth that can connect you back to a source of energy that existed in you prior to culture's impact on you, and the development of your own complex personality. Release the primordial wish inside you, feel it expand and grow. The more you do this, the more you will make direct contact with a giant urge. Just let the wish come out without shame.

As soon as it is completely there in the open, remove the images of your fantasy and remain only with the intensity of pure and raw power. Strip the thought away, and focus only on the feeling. Now you are in the presence of the force of creation as it expresses itself within you. Stripped of the specific contents of your wish, you can just feel the powerful sensation of wanting more, of expanding into everything and making it all yours. Your forbidden power-wishes only became neurotic when they were not allowed expression. But when they are carefully freed and brought to the surface as conscious parts of the psyche, you will feel more alive, more allowed to live.

Feel how deeply you are connected with this power until gradually you become calm and relaxed.

If you have not done the genie exercise yet, this would be a good moment to put the book down and do it; if by chance you are still reading on while in the midst of the exercise, we applaud your mental multitasking, and now is the time to close your eyes and just feel the energy coursing through you.

On the other side of this exercise you will be able to identify something sobering. You stripped away the specific contents of your primordial wish and connected it to the vast energy of life. Now when you think back and recall the specific details of your wish or wishes, you will probably find there is something laughable about your secret desires to control the world. You can clearly see the toddler in your grown-up self. If this is what is happening to you, then your will is entering the real world at last. This is the world where eight billion people live, each with their own will. Your will won't ever be the boss of all this, but it can be a part of it. You don't have to escape to a realm of fantasy. And that's a good thing. You can look around at the people in your traffic jam, your doctor's office, and in your home as well, and be aware of your will and the wills of the others. Now you are capable of seeing how essential it is to compromise if we want to live in a shared reality. You may want to be a dictator, but a real dictatorship is wretched for all but one megalomaniac (and it often ends wretchedly for him or her too).

Whenever you feel any frustration because of events or people blocking what you want, use that feeling to expose your primordial wish. If you put it into words, maybe even say it quietly to yourself, you can immediately recognize it as a fantasy: "My boss won't accept my idea. Doesn't she know I am a veritable font of brilliance? I want her to bow down before my superior knowledge whenever I speak!" Can you smile at yourself then? Once you expose your primordial wish, it loses its hold on you, and the frustration dissipates. But don't just let it go: that frustration is a reminder of your innate energy and power. It's just blocked off by the fantasy. Drop the fantasy, and the power behind it, the truly tremendous power within you, is all yours.

Will you find yourself saying…

"I just want everybody to get out of my way! Oh – there's my inner dictator, wishing to rule the world!"

"My partner doesn't like my idea of a camping vacation. Doesn't he/she realize that my *will* as supreme ruler of the universe must always be obeyed? I guess not. Oh well, in the real world maybe we should find something we both like."

"What do I really want? I want to be the most dazzling artist that ever graced the stage, leaving audiences mesmerized and enthralled. Okay, so now I can use the energy of this primordial wish to motivate me to get my first audition."

Chapter Four

The story of your life

You are invited to a party by a casual acquaintance. You don't expect that anyone else you know will be there. As you walk towards the house on the evening of the party, what do you feel? Has a chill of discomfort crept over your excitement as you knock on the door? You are about to enter unfamiliar territory. A half-smiling stranger opens the door. He looks you up and down as you stammer out that you were invited. The stranger casually waves you into the living room. A barrage of impressions hits your brain. The packed room, the hot music and the buzz of conversation all threaten to overwhelm your senses. Your body enters some subtle survival mode, becoming tense and alert. What's going on?

You're actually in the midst of a power play. Your mind is efficiently scanning the room and making dozens of swift, mostly unconscious evaluations of the power tensions and hierarchies on display. You have only a moment to gauge the best spots for you to fit in. The position you will finally select is your brain's best answer to the complex question: where is my greatest potential empowerment, and where am I least likely to face a potential weakening? Over there, near the center of the room, you see a small circle of confident-seeming men and women chatting and laughing loudly. There are a several more subdued conversations going on in closed clusters around the edges. In the next room the lights are low and people are dancing. Here and there a few individuals sit disengaged from the others seeming bored, playing with a wineglass or flipping through their smartphones. Your brain is furiously calculating like a supercomputer, weighing the meaning of countless microscopic signals as you evaluate your options for fitting in. Now decide, quickly, what will you do?

Did you instinctively move towards one option? Did it feel like the "right choice"? If you are like most people, the answer is probably "yes."

Your brain doesn't work this way only at parties. It does it all the time. One of its most important jobs is to seek power and resist weakening, and it is very good at it. In Chapter Three we discussed how the primordial wish you were born with collided with an indifferent reality. This collision was like the Big Bang, which started an astoundingly complex universe. But your individual Big Bang started the formation of your complex inner universe – your personality. With every action and reaction in the world, more layers are added to your psyche, wrapping around your primordial wish for endless self-expansion.

Your primordial wish was to become the ruler of all – like wanting to be the "life of the party." But the party of life never gives you everything you want. Life can be infinitely more hostile to your expectations than the most uncomfortable party. So you had to look for alternative ways to fit in and to settle for lesser forms of power. The memory of your weaknesses when life forced you to make compromises has been deeply engraved in you. These memories formed the story of your inadequacy, a story that has become fixed in you. It's not a sophisticated tale. It is a fundamental and instinctual experience that leaves you with an overall impression that life has always been this way. For this reason, we call it the *primal narrative*. Of course, it is not true that life is this way or that way. But we each feel our primal narrative as if it existed prior to all known experiences. We tell ourselves this is "just the way life is."

Your primal narrative is a mixture of three major factors. First is the basic level of power with which you were born into the world. Second are your first significant encounters with the world in which your wishes were defeated, you were forced to settle for less, and thus your inadequacies were laid bare. The third factor is the unique way in which you interpreted your weakening. We humans are capable of an amazing diversity of interpretations of any event. For example, some people who lived in a war-zone found it traumatizing and debilitating. Others found it empowering, something that enabled them to develop courage, resilience, or compassion.

Going back to the uncomfortable party, when you entered that house, your mind calculated your ability to fit in according to your unique and deeply held primal narrative. Bluntly, we each tend to stay clear of where we failed in the past, and move towards where we succeeded in the past. Your mind reaffirms your story of inadequacy with every new decision and reinforces the protective shield that prevents you from feeling the pain of breaking again. In a nutshell: *Every encounter in your life gets filtered through the lens of your primal narrative.*

This interpretation has been imprinted upon you so strongly that you don't feel it as your interpretation. Instead, it feels like a basic sense that this is the way things are. Within this interpretation, you are constantly seeking your "proper place." Your primal narrative is always running in the background, unnoticed, yet influencing all your important choices and actions, filtering your every experience. Often this preference will show up as pair of opposites, that which you seek and that which you avoid, like your very own "day" and "night," "light" and "dark," "good" and "bad." You might be drawn to experiences that make you feel free, and adverse to anything that places limits on you. You might be drawn to solitary retreats in nature, and adverse to crowds.

Here is a simple exercise that can help you connect with your unique primal narrative. Take a few deep breaths to relax, then read the words below, completing the sentence on your own:

> *Ever since I can remember, my most basic experience of life has been...*

Did words leap out spontaneously? If so, this can be a great starting point. Bringing the primal narrative to the surface of consciousness does not come easily for most people. As a person matures, the mind covers up our basic sense of inadequacy, masking our weaknesses and making the primal narrative harder and harder to find. It is revealed sometimes through dreams, irrational anxieties and moments of extreme vulnerability. In such moments your brain is less efficient at hiding your sense of inadequacy. I (Tim) got a sense of my primal narrative in my twenties and thirties each time a relationship with a woman would end with a breakup. I would find myself in a place of pain mixed with relief. Pain that I had been rejected and yet relief that I could stop making sacrifices for the sake of the relationship. That "place" felt wretchedly familiar, and each time I would catch myself thinking, "How did I get back *here* again?"

Another way to dig up your primal narrative is to look into your childhood memories. When you do this, focus less on specific events and more on the *general feeling* that connects them all like a subtle thread. Look also for the ways you reacted to these events: are there some persistent interpretations and conclusions? Is there some similarity in the way they all, or at least most of them, made you feel? Generally the best memories to search are the ones when you were between the ages of seven to twelve. This is usually the point in childhood when one's excitement of life has diminished and one has started to grasp life's cruel limitations. So refining the sentence we started with, you can complete this new version:

> *When I was between the ages seven to twelve, my most basic experience of life has been...*

Try to catch the most basic struggle or tension that runs through your childhood memories. What words best describe the clash between your wishing self and the reality of the world? For example, I (Shai) describe my primal narrative like this:

"Ever since I can remember myself, I have always had the feeling that I can never belong to anything in this world. When I was a young child, I felt I didn't belong to my body, my gender, my gender's sexuality, my family, my ethnic group, town, school, religion and nation. Even my very humanness was not easy to identify with! My inner myth was similar to Superman's who was sent from a crashing planet and remained ever since to hover over the earth. It was as if I had no place to rest my head."

If you turn this feeling over, it reveals a series of primordial wishes:

"I have always hoped for my dream world, a world which I fit in. In this world I get the body I want, the culture I like, and the family I wished for. My basic 'day' and 'night' of it is belonging versus not belonging. My weakening is the frustration of my primordial wish to feel part of an entirely made-up reality."

I (Tim) found my way to my primal narrative while writing a book that required some deep psychological excavation of my early childhood. I recalled my early school years as being haunted by a sense of exile, as if being sent to school were a punishment. The myth that resonated for me with this feeling was of Adam and Eve being chased out of the Garden of Eden for their sin. I felt as if I had done something wrong, and that if only I could be good enough and smart enough, I would somehow be allowed back in. My parents tell me I was a good child, always eager to help, and I sense behind their perceptions my terror of rejection. I wanted to be good, but feared that I was bad. Exile from Eden, and the search for the way back, in the face of my unworthiness – this was my primal narrative.

There are many types of primal narrative, each of which describes some form of inescapable inadequacy. You may feel that your search is for belonging, or for self-worth, or for safety, or for visibility in the world, or for the breaking of all limitations. Your own special search, whatever drives you in life, is powered by your primordial wish. Yet this search is bound to be difficult, since the world doesn't bend to your will. The world wants to be just as it is. More than that, the world wants to make *you do what it wants you to do, and be what it wants you to be.* Essentially, your primal narrative captures the tension between what you would like to be and what the world seems to force you to be.

Why is it so important to get hold of your primal narrative? It's because this narrative is the seed from which the entire tree of your personality bursts forth. The way you tell your basic story of life in the world determines every reaction and every choice you make. If the roots of a tree are unhealthy, the entire tree becomes sick. In the same way, if you manage to solve the tension and the quest at the core of your narrative, this will resolve the fundamental conflict of your psyche. Solving the primal narrative is the solution of the question of your life's journey. It's like starting an internal domino effect that calms the turmoil of your entire being.

There are two stages in the practice of uncovering the primal narrative:

The first practice is to identify and define it. This may take time. Don't push it. Enjoy the process of self-observation and contemplation. When you find some free time, sit down and write about your childhood and adolescent struggles with life and the world. To help you focus, answer each of these questions below:

What images of the world come up when you think of your early life?

Where did you feel inadequate and incompetent?

What were your first disappointments all about? Can you connect these to a strong desire that was shattered?

Who were your enemies and what did they represent in your mind?

What made you feel different from others?

What were your favorite mythologies? Were there heroes and heroines you identified strongly with?

This last question may hold a key for you. Each one of us is powerfully drawn to certain mythologies, not only because of their enchanting stories but also because their "light" and "dark," or "power" and "weakness" reflect our own inner struggles. For Shai it was Superman. For Tim it was Spiderman. If you imagined you had a secret identity or dwelled in an alternative reality as a special, powerful person, you have touched your primal narrative. In today's world children often find their resonant mythologies in animated movies that bring fairy tales to life, or video games in which one enters a mystical, magical world and goes on a quest. Perhaps companies like Disney and Steam know exactly what they are doing in building these longed-for fantasy worlds for children to escape into.

The second stage of recovering your primal narrative is retelling the story of your life. First write it all down just as you feel and experience it chronologically, without trying to improve and embellish it. For inspiration, draw on your answers to the questions from the first stage. You can also use these questions below:

What events and forces shaped your personality most of all?

How would you describe the way you evolved up to your present age?

What seems to be the central theme or unifying factor of your life story?

Describe the general feeling that follows this story.

Describe the general emotion that follows this story.

Describe the general thought that follows this story.

Give a headline to this story, just like in a newspaper.

After answering these questions, wait a few days before you return to your story. Give it some time to sink in. Next comes the crucial step. You are going to reread your story in search of the places where you feel a *deception of will hiding behind your negative emotions.* Just like the exercise you did in Chapter Two, you are going to take each negative emotion as a stone, turn it over, and find the frustrated will buried underneath it. Identify your buried will wherever you find it. For example, I (Tim) wrote that

I felt a "terror of rejection"; turning over that stone, I find a will to belong, to be accepted *unconditionally* exactly as I am.

Having identified each deception of will in your story, now rewrite it. Tell your true story as a walking ambition. Wherever you identify the primordial wish shattering in the form of great disappointments, pull it out and make it appear on the front stage of your life's play. Wherever past wounds and hurts are used to explain your innermost drives, emphasize instead your motivation to fulfill your will. Wherever you blamed someone or something for misfortune or turn of fate, rewrite it and declare your own expectation. It can be hard to let go of blame. But take into account one of the most important rules of this book: what you think makes you stronger, actually makes you weaker. Retelling your life in this way can in fact empower you. The original story, which bases itself on the sense of being life's victim, makes you feel like you have got no energy for life and for change. When your life story is rewritten – corrected, actually – you will discover that changing your past frees your present and your future as well. Both can become now unconditioned, raw materials out of which you can build a creative and exciting new life.

Will you find yourself saying…

"When I rewrite the story of my life, I can see that behind my resentment over my mother's neglect is my expectation that I would be loved unconditionally. Instead of blaming her, how can I use this powerful desire for love to build my life?"

"I really love this movie/book/video game. I wonder what character I identify with, and how his/her story resonates with my own primal narrative?"

"Wow, I feel really awkward in this situation, where do I fit in? My primal narrative must be kicking in. If I pay attention to what choices I steer away from and move towards, I bet I can better understand the story that unconsciously drives me."

Chapter Five

Those powers you will never have

What are your powers?

It's unlikely anyone has ever asked you that question. Maybe it's hard to think of yourself as powerful. But if we asked, "What are you good at?" a list of powers would come to your mind. Being good at something means finding an area in which you feel power and control. This includes more than skills, talents and attributes. Powers can also be your unique ability to feel deep intimacy with nature or to listen to angry people without losing your balance. The purpose of this chapter is to enable you to more fully own and feel those powers that are truly yours.

You, like everyone else, came into this world burning with the primordial wish at your core. You were overflowing with desire to conquer the world and make it yours. Imagine a mythical recreation of what this was like: the world, with its myriad options of power, is spread before you, enticing and inviting. You sense infinite possibilities, as if you were standing under a magic tree filled with golden fruits, and you only needed to take your pick of as many powers as you pleased. You could choose any of these:

- *The power of physical strength, skill or beauty*: the cultivation of your athletic performance or exceptional physical appearance. Can you think of times in your life in which you enjoyed the intensity of your body while performing or competing in a sport, or found yourself able to attract and magnetize others by your looks?
- *The power of belonging* to strong social structures: your family unit, your religion, community or nation, or even your favorite football team or rock band. Can you recall

moments in your life in which you felt the awesome power of some group consciousness, joining with thousands to cheer your team, or proudly singing your national anthem?

- *The power of the artistic expression*: reaching heights in your writing, painting, music, dancing or any creative endeavor. Have you ever felt that gushing energy that keeps you sleepless at night because of exciting ideas? Or the ability to mesmerize an audience with your talents?

- *The power of living on the edge*: the rush of thrill-seeking, risk-taking, extreme sports, or adventure trekking, "living dangerously" or feeling that you were flirting with death. This includes breaking social taboos in sexual experimentation or illicit drugs.

- *The power of competition and winning*: becoming the victor, the most famous, or the richest in your field, leaving all others defeated at your feet. Have you imagined winning prizes and trophies while the world applauds and your picture winds up on the front page?

- *The power of sex and sensuality*: the bliss of falling in love, intoxicating desire, the power of seduction and romance, the passion of sex, and the exquisite sweetness of lying wrapped in your lover's arms, as if the present moment contains all eternity.

- *The power of charisma and leadership*: influencing others with your ideas and words, perhaps even controlling and manipulating them. Can you recall moments in which you made a group follow you, or you managed some complex operation with people who trusted and obeyed your orders?

- *The power of the intellect*: philosophical knowledge, scientific brilliance, or innovative thinking. Have you ever tried really hard to solve a mathematical problem or to grasp a difficult text that, when unlocked, illuminated your understanding of life?

- *The power of practical ability*: building, designing, fixing, healing, cooking, and other powers requiring knowledge and mastery of the physical world and how it works.
- *Spiritual and religious power*: a special connection to the divine or universal force, unique visions, or the ability to perform ecstatic religious rituals. Perhaps you felt this power in your childhood when you visited church and were overwhelmed by all those holy images around you, or when you felt that God listened to your prayer.
- *The power to create, nurture and protect life*: to give birth, to parent, care for other beings, including nature. Parenthood is for some the most godlike power of all; you may also have felt it through teaching, caring for animals, tending a garden, or becoming an environment activist.

So, what would you choose? Take as many powers for yourself as you desire.

We hope you enjoyed this imaginative exercise. It is similar to the wildly unrealistic optimism of our early childhood. Back then you believed if you really wanted a certain power, if you really liked it, it would be yours. Perhaps you have childhood memories of becoming a prima ballerina, a professional football player, a movie star, or the president. Real life is not so easy. Indeed, you learned soon enough that life's powers were not simply yours for the taking. As a child you discovered your limitations. You were not the strongest, the smartest, the prettiest, the most talented, the winner, the leader, nor most favored by God. Painfully, you realized only a few could ever reach the top. You were *supposed* to be one of them, but somehow you were not good enough. You got kicked aside by an indifferent world and it shocked you.

A man in his forties told me (Shai) his vivid childhood memory of receiving this shock. As a young child he was an excellent runner and took great pride in coming first in cross-country races. But somewhere at the age of nine he became lazy and stopped training. He failed to notice that other boys were growing stronger, taller, and becoming more competitive. That year in the school cross-country run, others began closing in on his lead. He realized his days of easy victory were over. As they drew nearer, he felt his pride and confidence dissolve. In a desperate move he deliberately tripped, fell, and pretended to injure himself. He never raced again. This man's primal narrative revolved around issues of self-confidence and self-worth. So this memory became the perfect metaphor for his devastating loss of competitive power, and the deceptive way in which he dealt with it.

At a crossroads such as this, we are forced to make a *replacement*. When we realize we can't attain a desired form of power, rather than fail at it we replace it with some other kind of power. This is usually a less glamorous power, but one we can more realistically attain. The act of replacement often feels like a painful and bitter retreat. Like the young runner, we often turn away and never go near that kind of power again.

I (Shai) remember clearly my own moment of shock and replacement. It was my first basketball game at elementary school. I ran out with the other boys to the middle of the court, and the ball came at me. It hit me hard in the head. I reeled with the surprise and hurt of it. The sense of humiliation was so overwhelming that I made up my mind to never do this again. That was my last basketball game, my last competitive sport of any kind. Quickly I found my natural replacement: I retreated to proud isolation and reading difficult books. While the other boys were playing around, I felt superior to them because I was becoming intelligent!

I (Tim) had almost the reverse experience. In high school I became very good at math, winning school awards, and I imagined myself as a math genius, possibly making a career of it. I was also involved in other school activities and sports and was one of the popular kids. One of my friends, Lee, who did math competitions with me was rather introverted and unathletic. Math was his sole passion. In junior year he began to soar, coming near the top in provincial competitions. He asked me once what it was like for me to become totally absorbed in a math problem. He explained sometimes 12 hours went by while he was working on a problem, and then he would suddenly "pop out" into normal consciousness. I had to admit I had never had that experience. And I had to admit to myself that Lee was a math genius and I was not. I realized I was spread out over too many enjoyable "power forms" whereas Lee's introversion had helped him hone his one power into something magnificent. He won scholarships and went on to graduate studies in probability theory. Today, I'm lucky if I add up my sums correctly on my income tax.

A replacement is never our first choice in life, sometimes not even the second or the third. Did I (Shai) want to read books while all the other boys were playing? Not really. I actually wanted both: to be a confident basketball player *and* to be an intellectual boy. But noticing my different design, I preferred to avoid the really hard and humiliating competition and to withdraw to those places where I could be unmatched and untouched.

Frequently the most enticing powers we seek when we are young are the ones most clearly visible and tangible: success, popularity, admiration and control over others. This is only natural. Children learn quickly to evaluate and compare themselves with others, and to use the physical as a measure of self-worth and dominance. If you suffered from any defect, illness or physical difference in childhood, you probably were bullied, teased or excluded – events that forced you to somehow come to terms with a sense of weakening. Everyone would prefer to be both physically beautiful *and* internally beautiful. Being content with just inner beauty is a state of compromise. If you only could, you would have never made any replacement, just expanding more and more, adding new layers of powers, never losing anything on the way.

Some replacements are still external powers, like moving away from physical strength to intellectual achievements, while some turn more and more inward and secretive: technological skills replace physical strength, art replaces social acceptance, philosophy replaces leadership, and manipulation replaces beauty. Generally, people have a tendency to retreat inward and find their replacement powers in realms away from external measures of success and failure. In ages past, such a person might be a reclusive writer who never publishes her works, or a Buddhist monk who goes off to meditate in a cave. In the 21st century we might think of a "gamer" perpetually wired to his computer, whose avatar wins virtual battles, attaining the most advanced levels; or someone whose sense of power depends on the number of their Twitter followers or Facebook friends.

For most of us, childhood is when we face our most brutal power losses and find our major replacements. In adolescence we may retreat further inward as a stance against an indifferent world that denies us what we want. If we are fortunate, we find a few power forms we are good at which can help us to thrive as we move into adulthood. But the process of replacement continues through life, especially in our careers, relationships, and lifestyles. Older people must also deal with the loss of the powers they had when they were younger. The competitive gymnast becomes a coach; the washed-up celebrity becomes a charity spokesperson; the ex-president writes an autobiography and does a book tour. The necessity of replacements never ends, and some of these transitions are bound to be painful, even traumatic as we age and our powers decline.

What were the replacement powers you had to make in life – the compromises you settled for because you could not get the powers you wanted most? It may not be easy to be honest with yourself about this. Since we are programmed to want everything – to be beautiful and smart, wealthy and good, strong and loveable – those forced retreats feel intolerably humiliating. We tend to cover up our replacements, pretending to ourselves they were our first choices all along. This cover-up represses the pain of it, but it does not get rid of it. As a result, it is only natural to feel some bitterness and disappointment come to the surface when asked to acknowledge where you did not get your first choice and were forced to settle for less. Yet doing so will bring you a gift: genuine self-acceptance.

The exercise below will enable you to reveal and deal with your replacements. The insight that follows will be worth it.

Make a list of your replacement powers in life, from the earliest to the most recent. Use the questions below to help you reveal the ones you have covered up. Think deeply and take your time with this list so that you can be completely honest with yourself:

What dreams or desires did you hope to achieve, but you had to let them go?

What areas in life did you have to acknowledge you were not powerful enough to dominate?

When you recognized you lacked enough power in each of these areas, what new power did you turn to in exchange for the one you lost?

If your replacements don't seem obvious, ask two further questions to help reveal them:

> *Recall your most traumatic moments of weakening in your childhood and adolescence. What did you replace those weaknesses with that made you feel strong again?*
>
> *Do you ever compare yourself with others and say, "I'm not as famous/beautiful/talented/smart as them"? What do you tell yourself that you have attained that they still lack?*

Your real work with replacements is to fully accept and even appreciate them. The replacement powers you have identified are *yours*. You cannot let go of them. But you can let go of your lingering disappointment and bitterness over them. To do this, you need to release the repressed longing for the "impossible" power forms that you did not get. Your primal urge to be the best, the strongest, the prettiest was not some preordained destiny that went tragically awry. We all wanted to be number one at everything. The struggles in which you relinquished your first choices helped you to peel off an unnecessary self-image – what you thought you *should* have been or *should* have achieved. Life *forced* the winnowing of your primal urge so that you gave up what was not truly your own. You may not have liked it at that time, but the process of making replacements actually helped you find your authentic capacities and inclinations.

There will always be others who are more powerful than you, others who seem to easily possess the powers you've really wanted. Comparing your powers with theirs only weakens you. Not liking who you are because you're focused on a mirage of what you didn't get makes you neglect your real potential. Instead, embrace your replacements. They help you discover your true self.

When dissatisfaction keeps you focused outward on the powers you don't have, you may overlook inner powers that you didn't realize you actually possess. One does not always have to struggle with the world to possess power. Looking inwards you may discover you have the power to feel intensely, to remain loyal to your own truth in the face of strong opposition, or to appreciate beauty wherever you find it. You might also discover you have the power to commune with other powers – even if you don't personally possess them. This can be a source of deep satisfaction and joy. For example, even if you can't paint like Da Vinci, you can commune with his genius through your appreciation of his masterpieces. Appreciating the powers around you, from nebulas to great thinkers, connects you directly with them. In this way, you are capable of enjoying the feeling of power, and all the riches of the world.

As a final practice for this chapter, write a new list of powers: the replacement powers that are truly yours in the external world, and the internal powers you have discovered you also possess. When you finish this list, keep it someplace where you can keep adding to it. This will help you develop an accurate sense of the self you are creating.

Will you find yourself saying…

"I really envy her success as a scientist, I feel that 'should have' been me. But I couldn't make it, and I chose being a lab technician as my replacement power. I guess I can either let it eat me up inside, or accept my actual place in the world of power plays… If that's not enough for me, well, what else do I desire that I can realistically attain?"

"Some day maybe I'll… Gosh, I'm still dreaming of the powers I want but don't have. Maybe I'm ignoring my real powers. If I appreciated them more, I might be happier in my life."

"Sure, my first choice was to be a professional opera singer. But once I got over my bitter disappointment that I didn't make it, I stayed connected with my deep love of singing. As a music teacher I've found genuine joy in sharing that passion with my students."

Chapter Six

The ultimate feel-good trick

When you faced a personal crisis, have any of your friends or family members ever tried to comfort you with one of these platitudes?

"It's what on the inside that counts."
"You deserve better than this;" or: "You are way too good for him/her/them."
"When one door closes, another opens."
"This crisis is a blessing in disguise."
"Things can only get better."
"One day all of your hard work will pay off."
"Your loved one is now in a better place," (in times of grief); or:
"Your loved one is watching over you now."

Obviously you've heard them, and you have probably said something similar yourself when trying to uplift the broken spirit of a suffering friend. This makes perfect sense, right? It's what good friends do. It's the oldest trick in the book to help someone feel better quick. We call it *compensation*.

The purpose of compensation is to help us cope whenever we experience a loss of power. Let's say for example that one day your boss calls you to his or her office and fires you. At first, frustration, helplessness and humiliation threaten to overwhelm you. You may give in at this point to feelings of depression and pessimism. But soon you'll look for a way out, a way to feel better with yourself in order to go on with your life. You need to somehow shake off that sinking feeling. How would you do that?

Short term, alcohol, drugs, wild sex, or dancing all night at a club may blur your aching mind. But when you recover, the sting of your defeat will still be there. Like blood cells that rush to mend a bleeding wound, your psychic forces gather around a psychological wound in the effort to remove the pain and make things right again. To restore your sense of wholeness and integrity you create an inner rationale that makes you feel and think you are empowered and victorious even when in reality you've suffered a loss of power.

Compensation works through the realm of imagination. Harsh reality tells you that you have lost your job and that you face a confused and chaotic reality. So you tell yourself, "I deserved better than this," or: "Now that this boring job is out of the way I can focus on my art." Or a friend comes and says, "Hey, it's all for the best, your dream job is probably right around the corner." In that inner reality, losing one's job can only make your life better. As you start to believe it, you feel good again. You feel that you haven't been truly damaged, and that in fact your life is on course to a better future than the one that was ripped away from you. What a neat trick.

There's an example of this from the ancient Greeks. In Aesop's fable, "The Fox and the Grapes," a hungry fox saw a bunch of grapes growing high on a branch. She jumped and jumped, but could never reach them. In the end, exhausted and defeated, the fox walks away. But as she gives the grapes one last look she says, "Those grapes looked unripe anyway. I'm sure they were sour. I'm so lucky I didn't eat any!" The hungry fox created an inner reality that made her feel fortunate she did not get what she desired. From this 2,500-year-old fable we get the saying "sour grapes" – and a sense of just how old the art of compensation must be!

Compensation is often at work during a replacement: when you were denied some form of power you were striving for and then found a lesser power as a substitute for it. If you lost your job, you would seek another one as a replacement, or perhaps create one of your own. The replacement would definitely alleviate some of the pain and humiliation of your previous defeat. But not all of it. The stinging feeling would still be there, lurking in the dark. Compensation acts as a pain reliever of the psyche, creating mental, emotional and sensual means to form a conviction that your weakness was really an empowerment! In this way, for example:

"I cannot keep my job" turns into…
"I didn't want to keep this job anyway," which then turns into…
"It's fortunate I lost my job. It was the best thing that could have happened to me!"

Your loss of power becomes an advantage, an opportunity, and even a source of pride. You avoided "sour grapes!" You replaced the rejection and denial of the outer world with a self-approving, self-encouraging, but self-created environment. This is of course not the same as coping with reality. It's more like a bypass. You get to have your own internal world, which cannot be put to the test by anyone and anything. How did you learn how to do this?

You'll recall from Chapter Five that the most significant replacements typically happen in childhood and early adolescence. At this time in our lives, each of us had to make bitter compromises between our primordial wish to be all-powerful and the need to find our true position in the hierarchy. Our young minds could hardly be expected to endure the inevitable pain of weakening, and so we invented compensations to retain a part of our proud self-image and to escape from life's harsh realities. Some of these childhood inventions are profoundly imaginative. How about your childhood? Did you become attached to a doll or a blanket or toy that became for you a symbol of power or comfort? Did you invent an imaginary friend to be your loyal and wise adviser, like Calvin's tiger, Hobbes, in

Bill Watterson's famous comic strip? Perhaps through prayer you could summon God or his angels to magically help you. Some of us developed fantasies that we were somehow born into the wrong family, and that our real family was going to come some day and take us back to the palace where we belonged.

For most of us, our parents taught us compensations. Did your mother or father ever tell you when you lost a sports match: "Cheer up, you're still better than the other side – you've got great team spirit that they could only wish for"? Or when you were heartbroken after your boyfriend or girlfriend rejected you did they tell you: "S/he wasn't good enough for you anyway, you can do better." Or if you failed in some endeavor, "Surely God has a better plan for you." And as an adolescent, if you gazed into the mirror and hated how you looked compared to the more attractive and popular teens, did your parents point out your inner beauty, or tell you that for them "you will always be the most beautiful child on this earth"?

Your parents meant well, trying to shield you from painful feelings and boosting your young and fragile self-esteem. They knew what you did not: that life comes with unwritten and undeclared terms. No one asked you to sign the contract. It was signed without your permission at the moment of your birth. You got no say in the terms, and the life you were born into is almost completely out of your control. So the strategies of compensation seem like a clever way to opt out of this unfair world and into another world of fantasy in which we make all the rules and we will always win.

The resulting law of compensation is simple: *the weaker you become in the outer world, the stronger your inner world grows in compensation.* The inner world becomes your most reliable source of self-recognition and self-encouragement. This is not always bad. As well as children, adults in extremely stressful situations such as war can find compensations crucial for their mental health. Many forms of therapy employ compensations under the assumption that if people feel better about themselves, it can help them cope. Indeed, some individuals have even transmuted their inner world of compensations into paintings, poetry or other forms of great art, and that has value.

So what's the problem with compensations? In truth, if you don't know about *inner power*, why *not* make yourself feel better? The answer is that compensations always come with a heavy cost. We recognize compensations as *false inner power*, mind-tricks that provide pain relief. Like morphine, they numb you and make you feel good, while in fact they further incapacitate you. Compensations cannot resolve the basic tension of your life between your will and your fear of your own weakness. They cannot give you any real power.

Compensations disguise themselves so that you don't see them operating in your own consciousness.

Try this thought experiment:

Think of your thoughts and emotions as like a compensation factory in your mind. Imagine visiting this factory floor as an outsider, as an external inspector. Observe what exactly those invisible factory workers are trying to do as they diligently create your conscious thoughts and emotions. Wherever events and actions went against what you desired, they reworked your largely unconscious feelings of helplessness and powerlessness into a mental, imaginary world in which you had the illusion of control. Part of their job is to stay out of sight, as if they worked behind a curtain. In this thought experiment, you are trying to see behind the curtain. At first you'll only glimpse fleeting thoughts and emotions as they gleam and disappear in fractions of a second.

To help you with this mental inspection, here are examples of your inner factory's finest products:

- Whenever you deal with serious challenges that feel overwhelming, your thought offers some ideas of mental empowerment. For example, if you suffer from stage fright then before a presentation or performance you might get comfort from telling yourself that everyone in the audience loves you, or you might use the old trick of imagining the crowd is naked.

- If you have been physically endangered, you find a magical way to make yourself safe. So if you suffer from a fear of flying, while in the airplane you imagine that you're protected by angels, or that God won't let you perish because he has a plan for your life, or that through reincarnation you will be reborn, so you can't really die.

- When you need to cope with a serious disease, sudden abandonment or death of a loved one, you find some meaning in your suffering. If it's caused by Karma, for example, there's at least some point in your agony. Or if it's "in God's will," then it is part of some greater plan and the "reason" for your suffering will be revealed some day.

- When you have been hurt by life and people, your thoughts may create an inner sanctuary that can never be invaded by the outside world. It's like a dark corner in thought where you can escape life's brutality and feel unaffected and unbreakable.

- When you have been betrayed, abused or abandoned, your thoughts can turn the hurt into a source of pride and independence. If you're deceived by unreliable people in romance, work, or family, you can tell yourself: "My independence makes me strong; I don't really need these people."

- Whenever you want something badly, but you can't attain

it in the real world, your thoughts offer up the fantasy that you got it. A young man might get cut from a sports team and yet keep imagining over and over scoring the winning goal and being carried on his teammates' shoulders as the hero. An ambitious woman might fantasize about one day becoming the boss, even as she is passed over for promotions repeatedly.

Can you see in all these situations how compensations enable you to detach from what is actually happening? Compensations draw people's energy inwards, sapping their ability to act in the real world. We know you don't like feeling weak. Neither do we. It's natural to want to only experience what makes us feel strong. Compensations seem to offer an easy way to avoid feeling weak, and so they are very hard to resist – as hard as drugs for a junkie. And why resist if all that awaits you is the pain of your weakening? The journey to inner power gives you a reason to resist. In fact, it offers you a completely different path. Resist succumbing to compensation and instead *agree to fully experience your weakening*.

Accepting the moments in which you are weak will make you far stronger. This is the secret of really powerful men and women: they do not need to defend themselves, so they are less inclined to use compensations. They have learned how to use their weaknesses as a lever that helps them to advance and increase their strength. Behind this secret lies a very simple principle: as long as you're afraid of the experience of weakening, you cannot really live. It's meaningless to crave power-experiences without agreeing to pay the price of a possible weakening. It is only the primordial wish that hopes that somehow you will never ever lose a power play.

Agree to the weakening when it comes to you. Embrace it wholeheartedly as a natural part of life. Then you will no longer require compensations. Rather than escaping to a fantasy land in which you never lose the upper hand, keep standing there in the midst of defeat and admit it: "Yes, now I'm on the weak side of life." Once you do that, you can use this moment of weakening as the first step to true inner power. Just as a martial arts master turns the energy of her opponent's attack back against him, you will find ways to transform defeat to your advantage. You will find yourself saying: "So, what do I do next?" That next step is always a creative response, always flowing, never retreating. When true inner power is building in you, you will realize that compensations seem ridiculous and petty. You will feel strong at your core, at the depths of your being. In the later part of the book you'll learn how to build this strong core. For the present, start by welcoming moments of weakness as legitimate visitors in your life.

As you practice welcoming weakness, see if you can notice the workmen behind the curtain immediately starting to manufacture a way to make you feel better. Caught in the act, they will most likely put down their tools and quit. Next, notice if something begins to shift inside of you when you let go of your need to always have the upper hand. Do you like how this feels? Doesn't it feel strong? How strange is that? Accepting a weakening makes you stronger precisely because you are no longer pouring energy into your compensations. You are living in the real world, not generating a fantasy. Finally, tune in to the reactions of others who witness your power loss. Intimate friends might be surprised, even shocked by the change they see. You might notice them bracing for your reaction to your momentary weakness. Is this change in you a pleasant surprise for them? What comments do they make about it? Do they like it when you can admit a minor power loss and just move on with life? Do you?

The Psychology of Positive Illusions

In the past few decades an interesting body of scientific research has emerged on cognitive biases – the ways in which our minds systematically fool us into misperceiving reality. One cluster of these misperceptions is known as "Self-Enhancement Biases." These biases provide us with positive illusions of ourselves as more competent, luckier and better than others – in other words, they reveal the mind at work creating compensations. Here are the four main biases that psychological researchers have studied and named that make up this cluster. See if you can recognize any of them in the people you know – or in yourself:

Illusory superiority bias: The tendency to form an unrealistically positive view of yourself. Quick – are you smarter than average? Congratulations. In studies on this question, most people think they are smarter than average too. Now rate your attractiveness on a scale from 1–10. What's your number? In one experiment, researchers at UCLA conducted a survey of 25,000 people from 18–75 years of age, asking them this question. Most people rated themselves a 7. Fully one third of the participants under the age of thirty rated themselves a 9. You see the problem.

Illusion of control: The tendency to attribute good fortune to our own skill. Gambling is a great example of this. When you win at games of pure chance, you don't just feel lucky, you feel in control, as if it is something about you that is making the dice or the cards fall your way. You can also sense this when politicians from rich families – people who had their education, employment, and health benefits handed to them – opine about how poor people are just lazy, and should not be coddled by the government.

Optimism bias: The tendency to believe everything will work out in the end. We can smoke and won't get cancer. We can ride a motorcycle and not wear a helmet, and we won't get in an accident. We can break the rules and not get caught. If we suffer a loss, good fortune waits for us right round the corner. This bias disappears the minute we look at other people – we know they are idiots for trusting their luck. *We* are the lucky ones.

These three biases are reinforced by a fourth more comprehensive bias:

Confirmation bias: The tendency to notice and remember events and information that match your beliefs, and to ignore the events and information that conflict with your beliefs. As a result, whenever you win or things are going your way, you'll attribute the success to your amazing skills. But if you lose, that conflicts with your positive view of yourself, so you tend to focus on external factors – a late bus, a poor night's sleep, bad teachers or bosses, or teammates. Over time, the events that don't fit with your optimistic perception of yourself will fade away, and you mostly remember your successes, forming an inaccurate overall perception based more on your illusions than reality.

Will you find yourself saying…

"I'm overwhelmed and don't know how I'm going to cope with this loss… There *must* be a reason for it… Oh yeah, that's the workmen in my head manufacturing a compensation to try and make me feel better."

"'I deserve better,' you say? Thanks for the offer of mental morphine, but I plan to stay in the real world and just deal with what I have to do next."

"I can't believe I just failed. I guess it's my time to welcome weakness. If I can fully experience how this feels without resorting to compensations, I know this will make me stronger, and that's what I really want."

Chapter Seven

Revenge is not so sweet

I (Tim) have a shameful memory of watching a boy in my middle school class being beaten. I looked out a third story school window, and saw the boy curled up in a fetal position on the schoolyard below as a bigger kid kicked him. The boy had won a role in the school play, and I was cast as his understudy. I grew to dislike everything about him, and when I saw him being beaten, I just watched feeling a peculiar and ugly joy that I had never admitted before. The bully was, mystically, carrying out my revenge against this boy who had *taken my part*. How fortunate, I thought, if he is hurt too badly to perform...

Was there a time in your life in which you promised yourself to get even one day with someone for something he or she did to you? Even if you cannot recall something vivid right now, it is very likely that as you read this chapter a memory will come back to you. Such memories are sometimes locked away by your psyche. In part this is because the feeling of revenge is not considered moral, and partly because we make the promise of revenge so swiftly – sometimes in fractions of a second – we may be barely conscious we are doing it. The impact, however, can last a lifetime.

The *vow of vengeance* or *revenge-wish* is the third consecutive reaction your psyche may take in response to a significant defeat in one of life's power plays. Just like *compensation* (the second reaction), the role of the vow of vengeance is to alleviate the pain of *replacement* (the first reaction). But unlike compensation (which aims to make you feel better through retreating to an inner world), a revenge-wish tries to do the same by locating someone or something to blame for your power loss and promising oneself to give them a taste of their own medicine one day.

This promise alone is experienced in the psyche as a reassuring satisfaction. Since it also gives you a sense of strength and overcoming – "Perhaps you have the upper hand now, but just wait and see!" – in a way it can also be considered a compensation. However, a wish for revenge is more like an obsession with something external that seemed to be the cause of your suffering. It *waits* as if lurking in the dark, actively seeking the right moment to strike and restore your lost power. Do you recall Inigo Montoya, the revenge-driven swordsman from *The Princess Bride*? The meaning of his life was in delivering his line, "Hello, my name is Inigo Montoya. You killed my father. Prepare to die." In our lives, of course, we can't draw our swords to avenge ourselves. Sometimes we can take outward revenge, but sometimes it goes inwards, waiting for suffering to befall our target while we merely stand by and watch with glee.

Here are some of the ways we seek our revenge. See if you recognize yourself in any of them:

- Making someone suffer from precisely the same humiliation they inflicted upon you. This is like the biblical "eye for an eye." For example, if a friend makes you look stupid in front of others, you will seek out an opportunity to do the same back to them.
- Making others who never caused you any harm stand in for your original target, and making them suffer. Think of a man emotionally wounded by his mother who gets back at her by emotionally torturing his girlfriends.
- Making yourself stronger than those who made you feel weak, like the class nerd, mocked by his classmates, who becomes a powerful tech-company owner worth billions; he imagines his satisfaction when one day one of his former tormentors comes to him seeking a job.
- Watching those who weakened you become weak. Think of the delight some women take in a rival gaining weight!

Or the satisfaction of a manager, after losing a promotion to a young hot shot, who then watches that person screw up, crash and burn. There is an undeniable forbidden pleasure when your enemy suffers misfortune, even if we often won't admit it out loud: "Cancer? It serves him right."

- Finding a stronger person to avenge your suffering. You probably got your revenge this way as a child by "telling" on your siblings, then watching your mother or father punish them. At work, you might insinuate to a superior that one of your rivals is messing up, and then smugly watch his or her humiliation.

- Praying for God to be on your side and smite the wicked! Or course, the wicked tend to be those who inflict suffering on you. The Bible is full of injunctions that such evildoers be struck down in the present or punished for eternity in the afterlife.

You may not like to hear it, but chances are that you are right now in the midst of a lifelong journey of revenge, even if you are not aware of it. Something that someone told you or did to you – an insult or a slap – at some point in your life could have become the driving force behind the tremendous efforts you're making right now to succeed in your work or in a romantic relationship. Unknowingly, your entire effort might be dedicated to refuting that humiliating moment. For example, I (Tim) used to cringe as a boy whenever my father would call me a "clot" – an old British word that meant "clumsy" and "stupid." I often wondered if this motivated me to excel in school. I collected awards and trophies and displayed them on my desk at home. I still vividly recall the thrill I felt the day I finally beat my father at chess. Strangely enough, a Scottish author I know told me *his* father also called him a clot. The title of his first book? *Full Spectrum Intelligence.*

It could be also that an insult from a failed romance is

propelling you to prove that your life, after all, is not a failure. Or that climbing up the ladder of success is something that you do just to become eventually stronger or more impressive than some perceived rival. Such nearly unconscious vows can become driving forces in your life. The career you choose, relationships you value, the lifestyle and goals you pursue, the very things you think define your truest inner self may actually be rooted in a revenge-wish without your knowing it. This idea might be hard to bear. We like to think that our choices and actions in life are rational and spring from our true nature. But if you agree to take a deeper look and follow this chapter through to the end, you will be able to unmask your revenge-wish and put it aside. Then you can get to know your authentic self.

How can you trace the vows of vengeance that you took in your life?

The first stage is to ask yourself these questions:

"Who or what hurt me deeply?"

"Who or what made me feel humiliated?"

"What events and people made me feel even briefly as if I lost my power?"

Just sit for some time and let your memories slowly surface. Take a look at both your near or distant past. Make a list of at least ten occasions. Each such occasion holds within it a vow of vengeance. Here's why: *At every point of weakening in your life, you will find a secret or conscious vow, since your psyche immediately looked for someone to blame, and then alleviated the pain through the promise to "give back" this burden of weakness to the person who gave it to you.*

The second stage is for each of the ten occasions on your list: to locate the one who weakened you in each occasion, and then look for the fleeting promise you made to yourself to get even with the one who weakened you. Write these promises down.

The third stage is to examine carefully what courses of action and important direction you've taken in your life in order to fulfill each of your revenge promises.

When gathering these recollections, make sure you delve deeply into childhood and adolescent memories. These memories are packed with vows of vengeance, which have most probably determined the entire course of your life. Revisiting events of intense weakening in your early life can be painful. Look for humiliating situations in front of your parents, when they robbed you of your wish-fulfillments, or in the classroom in front of a mocking teacher or children, or in your first romantic disappointments and disillusionments.

I (Shai) will share as an example a session I once had with a thirty-year-old man whose lifelong obsession with the father figure was apparent throughout his entire biography and emotional reality. He was a bright young man yet he suffered from great insecurity and the need for some reassuring fatherly authority that would "show him the way." When we looked together into his early life, he immediately brought up a memory that had haunted him for almost fifteen years. This may sound like a petty memory, but in his mind it turned into a powerful metaphor. At the age of fifteen he had offered his father help in the kitchen. His father had asked him to bring him the spaghetti package from the cupboard. So the boy had pulled the package out and some of the noodles had fallen on the floor. His father had taken a penetrating look at him then twisted his face with disgust: "You really can't do anything right, can you?" These few noodles and the disgusted face of his father left such an impression on this young man that ever since he became desperate to correct his father's impression. He got entrapped in the promise he gave himself that one day he would prove his father wrong and would receive his father's approval. At the same time, his revenge-wish led him to wishing to one day look down on his father and prove his lowly stature, as if to say: "You're so pathetic I don't even need your approval."

I (Shai) have found working with hundreds of people that most are driven to some degree by the type of vow of vengeance held by this young man: *the promise that one day you will prove to whoever doubted your skills and abilities that you are not the loser and the nobody they thought you were.* It is a painful weakening when you feel your "true" value is underestimated or overlooked. Don't be embarrassed if you find this kind of vow in yourself. Many people's drive for success and self-fulfillment is fueled by exactly this sort of promise. It might not seem like a bad thing. After all, some people achieve a lot with this drive. But, it is such a powerful catalyst for ambition that it can make people uncompromising, uncaring and even violent in their attempt to prove their own worthiness.

Sometimes the person who caused the initial hurt has even left the scene or possibly died, yet the vow goes on: The elderly tycoon continues to amass a fortune to avenge himself against schoolmates who made fun of his poverty. The person who has raised a happy family envisions the lover who rejected him or her long ago showing up on the doorstep, lonely and broken-hearted.

Aside from the vow to prove we are not "losers," there are many other types of revenge-wishes:

Intellectual revenge: Proving that you are smarter than the ones who humiliated you in your weaker fields of life.
Spiritual revenge: Reaching internal heights that your enemies could never possibly reach.

Gender-revenge: Controlling and manipulating someone from the other sex to avenge some abuse or past insult.

Revenge of financial success: When a poor person becomes richer than those who once were his or her superiors, thus forcing them to respect him or her.

Revenge of independence: When a person proves he or she can live without the support of a parent, mentor, or some other authority.

Though all these revenge-wishes may be powerful motivators, they come with a heavy cost.

First, even the most glorious revenge fulfillment is just an attempt at regaining your power that was taken from you. Ultimately, it's driven by the past. Remember the lesson from Chapter Six: *waging battle against moments of weakness only makes you weaker.* You don't really get any power back from revenge, just the excited feeling you derive from your vow being fulfilled. It's an infantile fantasy that only soothes the part of you that can't stand the memory of defeat and failure. There is no *true inner power* in any of this.

The second problem with the "drive" produced by revenge is even more significant. In the third stage of the exercise above you were asked to bring up ten memories of past hurts and humiliations, search for the vows of vengeance that followed from them, and then look for the subtle ways in which these vows have shaped your life. Now look deeply into each one of these events and their ramifications in your life. Ask yourself: "Is this direction that I've taken really my authentic expression or have I become so caught in the effort to retaliate that I no longer live *my* life?"

Are you, instead, living your life on a course determined by a person who hurt and humiliated you, perhaps someone you even despise? It is the very nature of revenge to keep you focused on your target. Revenge keeps you chained to the person who hurt you. It weakens you for much longer than needed and lets that person hold you for the rest of your life. The time and energy you spend on your revenge-wishes are in essence given over to your enemy. This time and energy could have been yours, and now they are gone forever. So you need to let go of revenge not because of morality and religious forgiveness but simply because it's an astonishing waste of your own energy and potential.

In the end, revenge hurts you worse than it hurts your enemy. Revenge works against your true self and its true inclinations, against the life that you were meant to live. Sometimes people are so caught up in the obsession of revenge that they lose touch with their own natural drives. For example, they choose careers in order to prove something to someone, while neglecting their true talents and passions.

I (Shai) worked once with a very vulnerable, forty-year-old woman who admitted after few therapeutic processes: "My whole life was the defiance of male power, in the hope to show them that I too am able and competent." Ever since childhood, when she had discovered that she could not possibly be as strong as the boys, she had tried to measure up with them in various demonstrations of strength – choosing to play the guitar only because at that time in her scouts unit only boys had been playing the guitar around the fire, or deciding to become a squad commander of men in the army only to overpower male dominion. Even when she met me, she was constantly busy comparing her own power with the power of men around her, such as her ex-husband. Another man in his fifties realized through the treatment that he never got married or gave birth to a child only out of his lifelong revenge against his unappreciative father. By refusing to allow his father the continuation of his legacy and by depriving him of the happiness of a grandson, he felt that he retaliated for his father's misdeeds. Would these two people have lived totally different lives – their own lives – had they not been so obsessed with diminishing another's power?

So at the end of this exercise on revenge, ask yourself: "Is it really my life that I'm living or is my life being driven by someone else? If I lived without this vow of vengeance, would I be leading a different life?"

Will you find yourself saying…

"Of course I humiliated him. He deserved it. Wait a minute – was it really my *dead father* who deserved it?"

"Am I working hard for this career goal because I really want it, or because I want to prove to someone from my past that I'm not a loser?"

"I'm ending my vow of vengeance. I'm no longer going to live my life under the control of someone who once hurt me."

Chapter Eight

Hiding the bad and the weak

When you want the last piece of cake, do you grab it? No, you suppress your greedy urge and ask, "Would anybody like the last piece?" A "good" person wants just a little, never too much.

When a rival at work asks, "You seem a bit behind on that assignment, do you need some help?" do you reveal your fear about missing a deadline and accept the offer? Not likely. You say, "I've got it under control, thanks anyway."

When your spouse or romantic partner suggests you do an activity together that you don't like, do you answer with a straightforward, "No"? More likely you suggest a different activity, and you couch it in terms of what your partner might prefer to do – after all, you are only thinking of their happiness!

We speak in these strange ways because we all wear a social mask. Your mask is how you manipulate the perceptions of others so that they see you as you want them to see you and not as you truly are. We do this every day in a thousand ways. We can't help it. We have been trained by our parents, our teachers, our friends and our culture that give us our manners and morals. In fact the main point of manners and morals is to mask our unacceptable, willful urges and our constant engagement in the power plays of life. If you stand in the middle of the crowd and boldly declare your will, try to grab power whenever you can, and never consider the needs of others – as some people do – you might rise to the top as a dictator or business mogul. But more likely you will just find it hard to make friends, keep a job, or find anyone who wants to be with you. We wear the mask given by our culture to conceal our true face. We do it so that we can tolerate each other's company, get along, and cooperate in society.

As you mature in life your mask becomes like an elegantly sculpted work of art that you are constantly shaping for use in life's power plays. It becomes much more sophisticated than a mere cover for your desires. Your mask also includes anything else you've discovered that makes you more capable of getting what you want. So while some masks present extreme kindness and politeness, others take the form of exaggerated confidence, intimidating aggression, or pitiful victimhood (we will explore the latter in depth in Chapter Nine).

Because of this mask, you experience odd contradictions between what you express and what you actually feel:

You express admiration, while you're filled with distain and envy.

You obey, while you are filled with resentment.

You express respect towards a powerful leader or authority, while you long to rebel.

You say that you love someone, then when they displease you, you turn vengeful and violent.

You express friendliness and affection, while jealousy lurks within, waiting for an opportunity of weakness to take that friend down through gossip, sabotage, or abandonment.

You condemn miscreants who give in to their base desires, while inwardly you crave forbidden pleasures – and perhaps you fulfill them in secret. (Think of the surprising number of moralizing, anti-gay politicians and preachers who get caught having homosexual affairs.)

As you become more cultured and more refined, you discover you can less afford to expose your willful self: that second piece of cake, that wish to rebel, that hidden craving. A "good" person doesn't want too much, just a little. Only the uncouth, the bad guys, want explicitly, unashamedly and crudely. So one consequence of living with your mask on all the time is that you become habituated to thinking of yourself as powerful *enough* to play but never *too* powerful. Wearing the mask, you diminish yourself.

A brilliant new book by E.O. Wilson, the father of sociobiology, attempts to explain morality from a biological point of view. His theory explains the bind we feel when our mask forces us to diminish our power even as we inwardly long for complete expression of our wills. Wilson's thesis is that social insects – bees, termites and ants – are the most successful creatures on earth (in terms of total body mass, termites outweigh any other species on the planet). What is significant, Wilson writes, is that humans are the only non-insect life forms to have made the evolutionary leap to complex social organization – and we've done it in just the last 10,000 years. Wilson believes this is the reason for our dominance on earth today. Morality, he claims, is the social imperative that evolved to put the good of the "hive" before the selfish needs of the individual. If you look at what we consider virtues, he notes, our "good" qualities are all forms of service to others: altruism, kindness, honesty, fairness, courage, mercy, helpfulness, prudence, self-control… the list goes on. If you look at the vices, these "bad" qualities simply are the urges that promote individual survival and expansion: cowardice, greed, sexual indulgence, envy, cheating, boasting, and selfishness – just to name a few.

Of course, this is not what religions, social law and morality have taught us. For thousands of years, we have been taught that there's a *spiritual* battle going on inside us, a battle between two different parts: the darkness and the light, the good and the bad, the angel and the demon. This divides us within ourselves, and we come to believe that the bad part is something that must be repressed. The moral goal of these teachings? To attain a world in which good prevails over evil, where humans are all kind and fair and sweet all the time. Wilson, however, concludes something different. He believes humans will *never* become fully "good" creatures because we must balance these two opposing forces within ourselves: genetics drives us towards selfishness, while cultural training drives us towards promoting the group. Both good and bad are necessary, he concludes, in order for each of us to thrive as individuals living in society.

Wilson's theory is largely compatible with our perspective that people are walking wills. Our evolution as social beings has greatly expanded our species power, while at the same time creating more and more opportunities for individuals to express their personal power. However, Wilson's biological analysis affirms this basic dualism that leaves us paralyzed between the opposing forces of good and evil. This is because he looks at human evolution only from the outside. From the *inside*, we can look at human history and see that the good part in humans does not merely stand in opposition to the bad part. Instead, we see good as *emerging* from the bad part: the wish for peace is the result of tireless wars; the enlightened mind of the Buddha is the result of suffering and ignorance; the longing for true love springs from plain desire and infatuation. Morality itself did not just appear out of nowhere. It evolved from the conflicting and competing struggles of early societies as a wish for order, and the kinds of mutual agreements that allowed our ancestors to trust one another beyond their tribal clans. One very recent example of this is how Europe nearly destroyed itself in two World Wars in the last century, only to emerge in the 21st century as a peaceful European Union with values of tolerance, cooperation and collaboration.

The surprising insight from all of this is that your bad part is not the opposite of your good part. On the contrary, the good in you is the maturation and the transformation of your "evil" side. *Good evolves from bad.* The two don't flow from different rivers, one black and one white, that never merge. Instead they come from a common spring. They are not an angel and a demon each sitting on a different shoulder. The good and bad in you come from the exact same stuff: the raw energy of life that creates your urges and desires and your will. There is no moral dualism, just one continuum of energy that includes all the bits we label "good" and "evil."

From this perspective, it's vital to embrace and even love the evil within: the unkind, selfish, even wicked parts of yourself. The reason is simple: if you push them into the darkness and let them suffocate and die away, you end up having very little energy, and very little energy means very little inner power for growth and transformation. This view may frighten those who believe a firm moral code is essential for people to live together in peace. But we don't see this as a contradiction. One can accept morality as an intrinsic and necessary part of culture while still embracing the reality and value of all those untamed forces and energies that live inside you, behind your mask.

We believe the perspective that good evolves from bad opens new channels for authentic moral development and growth. This is because the raw material of the "bad," selfish, primal urges flowing in you is exactly what can create your most powerful, positive, compassionate, and courageous qualities. Your "bad" needs to flow without resistance if it is to stretch out and transform. This includes your murderous impulses and fantasies, the forbidden regions of your sexuality, and the secret hatreds and jealousies you have covered up that fester in your heart. The problem with conventional attitudes to morality is that by making "bad" into a metaphysical evil to be shunned, they stop up the flow; instead of transforming, you get energetically stuck and then become morally stunted. When obedience becomes the definition of moral, you are left "trying to be good" by living up to an imposed external standard. When the pressure becomes too much, the dam bursts and you act out your worst impulses.

I (Tim) experienced this in my first marriage. For three years I had struggled to rise above my wife's sexual frigidity as a spiritual, moral man. I had been completely invested in becoming my mask – to be good, not to want too much. Then something snapped and I became a different person, one capable of having clandestine sexual affairs. Suddenly I was living a Jekyll-and-Hyde type of existence. My hidden lustful, willful self was out of the cage. "It" caused a lot of pain to my family, my young son, and to people I loved. But the point to the story is that my "Mr. Hyde" began to evolve. It wanted *integration* with the rest of my life. Ironically, when I first met my second wife, Teresa, she found my willful, lustful self refreshingly authentic. Gradually this formerly shut-away part of myself has changed. "It" has become "me," and this once-twisted energy has turned into my capacity to love.

Where does this leave you with your own mask? The goal here is *not* to remove your mask and live a life of wild and willful abandon. I (Shai) often have people tell me in therapy they harbor the dream of one day becoming completely their "true self," expressing exactly what they feel and doing exactly what their urge tells them to do. As long as they don't get this ultimate wish fulfilled, they express a grudging sense of oppression. Sometimes this verges on the absurd: one young woman who loves participating in Shamanic rituals (in which people consume a psychoactive plant) got really offended one day when she came to visit her parents. Her father took her to the kitchen, and asked her gently not to mention these rituals while her aunt – a conservative and easily agitated woman – was also in the house. This woman used this story as a proof that her family wouldn't accept her true self! If you choose to be part of culture, you have to forgo the fantasy that the world will embrace all that your willful self wants to express.

The essential message of this chapter is to accept the compromise made between the primordial wish and culture. You want to wear the mask while becoming fully aware of who you really are behind it. *Wear, and be aware.* Literally make friends with your willful self, rather than seeing it as an enemy you must suppress or as an "it" that is somehow separate from you, not part of your complete nature. This exercise will strengthen you in integrating your willful nature into your sense of self:

This practice requires you to keep a notebook with two columns: one for your "bad" part, in which you will write down all your bad thoughts and impulses, and one for your "good" part, in which you will write down all your good deeds and impulses. After a week or two, read through the bad column and see if the items you have written there actually have a potential for something. Remember, your "bad" energy is abundant energy; it seeks direction and transformation. Can you accept that you contain that energy? Can you embrace it rather than block it off? How could you actually use that energy for further growth? Close your eyes for a minute and feel how these two forces labeled "good' and "bad" are actually one force running through you, gradually becoming pure energy and pure power.

Together with this reflection you can practice expressing your wills and desires more simply and honestly, letting others see behind your mask. Don't try to play games. Don't make others think that you say one thing while you really want another thing. You have to do this carefully: express yourself in a non-forceful way. Just express your will to let it be there, in the open, but don't turn it into a violent demand. This is about revealing your true face, not about unleashing your inner dictator! If you want sex from your partner, don't use elusive body language and don't create awkward situations just because you're afraid of the humiliation of rejection. Say plainly: "I have to tell you, I'm overwhelmingly attracted to you right now and I'd love to have sex with you." If you really need a hug from a friend, don't freeze out the feeling and become even more distant. Say: "I really, really need a hug right now. Would you be there for me for a moment?"

Now let's examine the aspect of your mask that pretends to show that you are strong when in fact you are weak. Think of this scene from a thousand movies: someone mistakenly or intentionally kills someone else, and then rushes to bury the body in a place unknown, usually in the dead of night, quickly before the police find out. That's why we call this second function of mask wearing, *bury the body!* When you're weak, you need to bury the body of your humiliating defeat.

What happens in a pack when the alpha wolf gets old or injured? The beta wolves challenge, attack and defeat it. Something in us instinctively fears this could happen to us if we were to reveal our weaknesses, our forced retreat from areas of failure. Looking too weak in a world of constant power plays seems dangerous. It's not as if you can never disclose even the slightest sign of weakness, but you definitely cannot be considered weak for too long. So your mask is not only an efficient way to conceal your wills. It also serves as a protective shield that helps you to pretend you're powerful enough to withstand the pressures and demands of life. This is why we expend a lot of energy trying to convince those around us that we *almost always* win, that we are walking a pathway towards success. And if we ever walked away it is because we quit the game, not because the game defeated us. Here's how we do this:

First, we cover the tracks of our replacements:

"It's not that I'm afraid of relationships, I'm just taking some time out for 'me.'" Or, "I'm pursuing a higher spiritual path," or, "I've chosen to devote myself fully to my career," or, "The people around me are too boring to interest me."

"They didn't fire me – I lost interest in my job long ago, and I wanted to be let go!" Or, "They didn't offer enough opportunity and I needed to move on," or, "This job was stifling my creativity, and now I can devote myself to my art!"

Second, we disguise our compensations so others will think they are a description of reality, and not just our consoling interpretation:

"I believe that my disease has a higher purpose as part of God's plan." Or, "I know that this disease plays a major role in my development and learning. It's the best thing that has ever happened to me!"

Third, we camouflage our revenge-wishes (in so far as we are conscious of them) so that they sound like reasonable corrections and a cosmic rebalancing in order to create a better world – and not a primitive desire for release through vengeance:

"I believe that when my father sees my forthcoming success, he will learn to appreciate the real 'me.' Then he will correct his mistaken view that I'm a disappointment. That will help us reach a new level of harmony and healing in our relationship."

With your mask firmly in place, you can appear dignified even in your worst moments of humiliation, confident in your most embarrassing times of frailty, and reasonable even when you're in your most irrational states. This is why, for example, some people turn to rage when they are exposed in their weakness. Rage is still an expression of power and it can serve to cover up their wounded self. I (Tim) recently came to grips with this in one area of my life: my sense of direction. I've travelled a lot, and

I pride myself in my sense of direction. Whenever my wife doubts me when we are driving or walking through a strange city, I get really offended, as if I'm an infallible compass. "How *dare* you doubt me!" is my attitude. The fact of the matter is, I am sometimes wrong: 180 degrees wrong. And when I am wrong, it is very hard to admit it, and so sometimes we wander for quite awhile, me insisting I know exactly where I am going even when I really don't.

So, what's the result of wearing the mask of power? You exert a lot of energy pretending that you feel what you don't really feel, and that you don't feel what you really feel. In the end, you end up thinking your powerful mask is who you really are, but inside you still feel you are weak (and in Tim's case, lost). You gradually detach from your actual reality: the reality of your will as well as the reality of your weakness. In this way, you can no longer be connected to your healthy willfulness and be simple about it. And since your mask is so busy denying any feeling of weakness, you can no longer get in touch with your weakness and learn from it one of the most important lessons that life has to offer.

This is how you can loosen the grip of the mask on your face and be more connected to the actual, vibrant you: use less manipulation and be more straightforward about your desires and defeats. When I (Tim) learned to admit to my wife that I'd lost my way, she never berated me. In fact, she always appreciated it when I dropped my infallible compass act, because then we could work together to figure out which way to go. So learn to acknowledge your weaknesses simply and honestly. Be careful: don't use this as an opportunity for further manipulation, to make people pity you. When you face defeat, just say it without making excuses for your failure. Here are four ways you can get started:

Concede an argument. Whenever you sense the person you are arguing with actually has a strong point, stop arguing. Say:

"Oh, I see what you mean. You are right and I was wrong. Thanks."

Admit losing hurts. If you are defeated in a game or a sport or suffer a setback at work, just be honest with the winner about how it hurts. "Wow, you really beat me badly. What a blow to my ego!"

Accept when someone refuses to do you a favor. Resist wheedling, arguing, guilt-tripping, or pondering what's gone wrong with the relationship. You are not the one with all the power, so accept it. "You don't want to help me move furniture? Well, I guess I'll find someone else."

Point out your own mistakes. Stop covering up for yourself, hoping no one will notice. Make no excuses. Accept the blame without defending yourself. "I forgot to file that report before the deadline. Sorry, this is my mistake."

Put these into practice consistently and conscientiously. They probably go against your habitual tendencies, so you will have to be deliberate about it. Notice when you say these things how this breaks the tension, and releases much positive energy that you now can use for other purposes. Also notice how those around you react. Do they find it more enjoyable to be around someone who does not insist on being infallible and invincible all the time? Do they actually like you better without your mask?

Will you find yourself saying…

"My mask says 'no,' but my will says 'yes.' But this is not a moral struggle that divides me into 'good' and 'bad' parts. How can I use this current tension to become more conscious of my willful nature – *to wear and be aware?*"

"I don't fool myself into thinking I'm a 'good person.' There's a strong will behind my mask, and I can use all that energy for inner power."

"Hey, can I tell you what I really want right now?"

"You were right and I was wrong. Thanks for pointing that out."

Chapter Nine

The eternal victim

What's the difference between Lord Voldemort from the *Harry Potter* series and the wizard Saruman from the *Lord of the Rings*? Both are evil, but they came from different literary times, and the nature of their evil is profoundly different. When Tolkien created Saruman in the 1930s, the idea of an evil wizard tempted by the dark side to achieve the ultimate degree of power made a lot of sense. Our collective belief-system understood that wickedness opposed goodness, and that was that. "But why?" you might ask. "Why would he be tempted? What was his motive?" You can search the whole trilogy and you won't find an answer. There is no "why." Saruman simply wanted infinite power. His primordial wish arose out of the darkness of his soul and grasped for it, openly and uninhibitedly. Indeed, he stands with a long line of profoundly wicked literary villains: Moriarty, Captain Hook, Iago, Dracula, Loki, Satan (from *Paradise Lost*) are all compelling characters in part because of their complete embrace of their wickedness.

Lord Voldemort, on the other hand, was a product of our present generation. He belongs to what we could call the *New Evil*. The New Evil always has a psychological reason for being bad. There's no primal wickedness, only a victim who was driven to become an aggressor. Trauma and deep-seated pain transformed this victim into a villain. In our modern belief system everyone is essentially good; villains are just good people who got twisted along the way. Accordingly, in the *Harry Potter* books, Voldemort was an orphan. His father abandoned his mother who died shortly after the baby was born. It was Tom Riddle's abandonment *wound* that shaped him into a monster.

Two other examples beautifully illustrate this sudden

psychologizing of the New Evil: Darth Vader and the Wicked Witch of the West. In the 1970s' *Star Wars* movies, Vader was pure, powerful evil (until his deathbed conversion). The 21st century trilogy focused entirely on the psychological wounds Anakin Skywalker, aka the young Vader, suffered as a child (his slavery, the murder of his mother), and how this suffering grew into fear, fear which the Sith Lord manipulated to lead the youth into evil. In *Wicked*, the relentlessly wicked witch from Oz becomes a sympathetic heroine: ostracized as a child for her green skin and driven to deeds of desperation by the oppressive wizard. Even comic book villains – Catwoman, the Goblin, Magneto – are given a traumatic backstory that psychologically justifies their evil.

The compulsion of authors and film producers these days to provide traumatic, psychologically sophisticated motives for their characters is entirely congruent with the dominant worldview of our age, Liberal Humanism. Liberal Humanism puts humans at the center of the universe, valuing above all else individual rights, freedom, and voice. While there is much that's good about this, it has also created a problem. Liberal Humanism takes humanity as fundamentally good, and places the psyche at the center of each human being. Thus the inner realm of our personal feelings has become sacred territory – an exceedingly fragile and delicate territory requiring endless care and protection, since psychologists have determined we are all wounded and broken souls driven by childhood traumas and pains. We don't want to offend anyone; we don't want to damage anyone's self-esteem; and we want to be compassionate about everyone's traumas.

Sensitivity is fine; but what has happened as a by-product is we have internalized the concept of the wounded self as if it were fundamental to human nature. In fact it is a very new idea. It has never been proven. Instead, it has merely become popular, repeated so often in our culture that it seems real just because you run into it everywhere. It's become a belief. You'll find it in therapy, self-help, alternative medicine, spirituality, art, entertainment and social movements, even prison reforms. As this idea is absorbed throughout our culture, it also becomes our individual habit of thinking. We analyze our patterns of behavior and wonder who might have hurt us, or what childhood misery might be at the core of our unhappiness. Why do you suffer or make others suffer? What memory lies buried in the depths of your past: something that somebody did to you – a relative or classmate? Your misery in life must be the result of some victim-experience that broke you. It's as if we have created a new human right for ourselves: the right to be a victim. And the purpose of your life? To delve into your trauma, rehabilitate your broken self, and heal your wounds. With this yearned-for healing, no matter how miserable or wicked you were, you will at last be restored to the good person you are at heart.

There are two logical problems with our belief that everyone's a victim, and one very practical one. First, if every person is a villain because of a childhood wound, then all their aggressors were themselves victims. It creates a line of victim dominos that goes right back to the origin of humanity. There's no first villain – so how did this get started – with Adam and Eve abusing Cain? Second, if all eight billion of us are victims, then there can be no actual villains in the world. If we deeply believed in universal victim mentality, we would have to completely give up on the concept of "villain." But we don't: to be a victim, you need an aggressor. Beyond pointing out the logical flaws in this way of thinking, practically speaking, believing your identity has been formed around your victimhood has strong negative consequences. Sanctifying the experience of the victim as the center of the psyche can cause you to hold on to your victim-identity, impeding your growth and development.

I (Shai) have grown accustomed to people coming to me after countless other therapy sessions clinging to their past wounds even more tightly than they had clung to them before entering therapy. When they begin our first session together, they immediately and efficiently pour out their sad stories as the reason for their present frailties and difficulties. Though they complain about weakness, they get pretty aggressive in their demand to be recognized as victims. I'm not saying that past events don't contribute to our personality formation. I'm only pointing out that these people hold on to their traumas and too easily identify with them, often as an excuse that releases them from responsibility for their own life and suffering. Everyone is busy forgiving their attackers and struggling to release haunting traumas. I'm amazed at the number of people who come to me with "traumas" they were only *told* about, like a birth trauma or an "unconscious" sexual abuse, or events that were not registered at all as devastating at the time that they happened. It became clear to me that people rearranged their narrative of the event according to what they wanted to remember, and telling it in such a way as to justify their basic position as victims. Even when people come to me to treat rage attacks, they always tell me how they were attacked in the past, and that this is what made them aggressive. Sometimes they go as far as claiming that when they attack others, they too are victims! In my past work with prisoners jailed for extreme violence and even murder, they often declared that their criminal acts had been caused by early traumas, as if they were the unfortunate carriers of some disease that forced them to behave in such ways.

But are we really just innocent and vulnerable creatures who got twisted by unfair traumas? Is it true that without traumas we would have craved no power, purely manifesting as love in human form? If you have sincerely followed the journey of this book, you doubtless can see why we reject the idea that your pains and sorrows should be considered the center of your identity or the focus of your life. Remember, *will precedes suffering*. Coming into life you are already a restless walking will.

Your story is not a story of a victim – it may include victim-experiences, but *you are not a victim.*

When you understand that you're first a walking will, you can see that being a victim in this world is only a temporary period of weakening, not a constant state of being. In a negative state, you are a frustrated and thwarted desire. If you only could, you would have immediately chosen to become powerful. But when you cannot, you bitterly pass through the journey of compromise: replacement, compensation, revenge and concealment. When a person comes to me (Shai) for treatment, and complains about their victim-position in the world, what they really mean to say is: "It's not fair that I was on the weaker side of life!" Indeed, it hurts badly for them to know their wills were defeated so completely, and that they could not fulfill their primordial wishes. This, and not victimhood, is the true face of their agony.

This is why we call the wounded self the *false subconscious*, and the willful self the *true subconscious*. The false subconscious is actually the most common type of concealment – a sophisticated disguise of the willful self. It's simple: you put on the mask of the victim to distract everyone's attention, including your own, from your true being that forever seeks expansion and enhancement. The role of the victim mask is to blur the real driving forces of your psyche.

Why would you need that? First of all, the victim mask justifies your negative behavior patterns, like an inability to hold a steady job or to commit to a loving relationship. Second, the victim mask enables you to keep on wanting without anyone noticing. This opens the way for you to manipulate unsuspecting others. Everyone who believes your mask will be convinced that you're a pitiful being that cannot really want. Your wishes will seem like necessary justice: it's only fair you would be compensated somehow for the past wrongs done to you. Third, the victim mask allows you to freely complain about the powerful others in your past or present, claiming that they are responsible for your tragic condition, not you. These three reasons make the false subconscious a very useful – but harmful – tool in the world of power plays.

In truth, the victim mask is just not realistic. To reverse an old adage: life weakens all of the people some of the time, and some of the people all of the time, but life does not weaken all of the people all of the time. Unless you are one of the unlucky ones – debilitating childhood illness, sex trafficked, living in a war zone – your sense of victimhood is probably distorted. Many people get *severely* frustrated and weakened at some points in their lives. But if you are living through the false subconscious, you will find yourself searching out those moments and collecting them, embracing them and turning them into an identity. Eventually you become so identified with the victim mask that you detach from your willful self, and then your will becomes a truly repressed subconscious – a vital part of your self that you have lost connection with.

When such people go into therapy, they choose to show the therapist only their false subconscious. Externally, it seems they are trying desperately to "heal" their wound. But that will only be a distraction: at the base of their true subconscious, their primordial wishes will remain intact but buried, unknown to both therapist and themselves. They will tearfully talk about their suffering and will demand from the therapist the right to do what they couldn't do in real life: express what they wanted but couldn't get. This distraction, emphasizing their victim-experience to cover up their aggressive attempts to get what they want, is called a *diversion*. The false subconscious is actually composed of countless diversions. Diversions enable a frustrated person to keep the focus on their victim-experiences, even when those experiences resulted directly from their own aggressive, unconsciously repressed will.

I (Shai) will give two short examples from my therapeutic

experience that will easily clarify the meaning of diversion.

First, a man in his forties who cheated on his wife for almost a year with her closest female friend came to me to complain about his wife's response: when she accidentally discovered this shocking truth – a revelation that initiated their gradual and painful divorce – she responded with rage. Amazingly, he wasn't at all troubled by his own cheating. He actually made himself a victim of his wife's aggression, complaining that she was insensitive and careless when it came to his own needs!

Second, another man in his forties described a childhood trauma from his days in elementary school. At one point his playmates banished him from the soccer field. He responded with shock and brokenheartedness. The true story, however, was the fact that long before the banishment he had attempted in every way possible to make himself king of the school. He had humiliated all the other children, doing everything he could to prove he was far superior to the rest of them. His moment of trauma was simply the moment in which all those children refused to tolerate his megalomaniac behavior.

In sum: *diversion is a manipulation that helps you ignore the cause and effect, and focus only on the effect.* It deftly shifts your identity to the victim in the story, while deeply burying your will. Your psyche invests in the feeling of the wretched victim because it replaces the unbearable pain of your defeat. And it helps you to draw to yourself the compassion of others (like those violent prisoners who shifted their attention from their acts of violence to their wounded childhood). There's nothing more liberating – and more deceiving – than to put on the victim mask when you get caught and start complaining about how you suffered at the hands of others.

The problem, of course, is that taking your few memories of hardship and suffering and crafting them into the mask of a victim becomes a trap. You get stuck with a self-image that can never be healed, and a life in which you are disconnected from direct access to your will and hence your true power. No amount of therapy will do you any good as long as it reinforces your wounded self, your false subconscious. You will be stuck with a life whose main aim is to pity yourself, and your relationships will revolve around gaining the pity of others.

If you resonate with this on any level, then here is your chance to shake off your victim identity once and for all. Just look around you and listen to how everyone complains all the time about life's unfairness. You'll get the point quickly: pitying yourself is only a collective habit that cannot empower you, only weaken you. You are not a victim of life in any special way. We've all suffered. We are all victims to some degree. If everyone's a victim, what's the point in making this the centerpiece of your identity? Ask yourself: am I using my story to pity myself or to justify my present position of inadequacy and suffering? Do you have the story of "pitiful me" down pat?

"My father left me at a very young age."
"I was sexually molested when I was seven."
"My parents divorced when I was ten."
"I was mocked or bullied through school."

These are truly painful experiences. They deserve compassion. But are you using them and holding on to them more than they actually hold on to you? Do you believe your wounds limit what you can and cannot accomplish today? Do they define your relationships? Do they *serve you* in manipulating others to get what you want? If you answered "yes" to any of these questions, then you are attached to your wounded self. If you want to heal yourself, you must cut the cord and let that victim-image go. Care for your wounds like you would care for a broken arm. Set the bone, then let it heal without reliving and retelling the accident over and over again.

If you still wish to seek therapy to heal some past wounds, go ahead and do it. Just make sure you find a type of therapy that will release you from the victim-identity and encourage you to assume full responsibility for your suffering. If your treatment is all about your "wounded-ness" and it focuses on your traumas as the source of your pain, then you are only feeding the false subconscious. *The wrong therapy can keep you weak forever.* Remember that behind the layer of pain there hides the layer of will. Search for a therapist who can look into your infantile wishes and deep aggressions, and who will not be distracted by your complaints about being a victim. Find someone who can help you let go of the false subconscious and your sense of powerlessness, and help you focus on ways to get better and gain what you want in life.

As a first step, try this practice:

Write down your sad story, or tell it to a loving friend or relative. While telling it, feel at first how it's heavily charged with the feeling of the victim. Then tell it again, sticking more to the facts and looking at it just like a memory you're recalling. Then tell it again, and again, until you feel it's not charged anymore; that it was just another experience. Then ask yourself sincerely: who would I be without the victim-identity? You will soon realize that you're finally able to take responsibility for your life. It's the victim-identity that makes you feel unable to take that responsibility now.

Be careful not to buy your own story of misery. This story obscures and diverts attention from your true story, the story of one who came to this life in order to always want more. If you clearly admit, "Yes, I want, sometimes even aggressively; this is my fundamental experience of life," you actually reposition yourself back to the beginning of your life. It's as if you have pressed a reset button. New questions will suddenly arise for you:

"What am I trying to achieve in my life?"
"What types of power am I striving for?"
"What were the obsessions that caused my misery?"
"What are my primordial wishes that refused to compromise and that I still expect the world to submit to?"

You can easily become your greatest therapist. Just stop treating your secondary emotions, like depression or anger, as if they were the heart of your being. Instead, start recognizing your stubborn struggles with reality as the expression of your true will.

Will you find yourself saying…

"Would you do me a favor? Would you listen to me tell you my story of victimhood? I'm tired of it, and this is a kind of therapy to help me get over it."

"I'm getting blocked again, not getting what I want. I can feel my story of 'pitiful me' kicking in. But I don't buy it any more. That's my *false subconscious* trying to divert my attention. What else could I do to get what I really want to achieve?"

"I used to be a victim, but I quit."

Chapter Ten

The shock of powerlessness

I (Shai) am always intrigued by the fact that people who come to me for therapy often recall their traumatic memories in an intentionally distorted way. They magnify their trauma. They narrate it in a way that justifies their self-pity. With self-pity the memory becomes disproportionate and distorted. As we reveal the complete picture of cause and effect in my sessions with them, new details suddenly appear to explain the situation in a totally different way. Of course this is quite natural since the brain's role is to faithfully stand beside its owners like a loyal dog and represent its case. Yet in our present times when the false subconscious rules, people will always present a fragile picture of their psyche to support their image of a broken self that forever needs healing. I think we are losing our sense of proportion of what is and isn't trauma. Some people come to me to heal them of traumas that frankly seem ridiculous: getting hit by a snowball, receiving a sour look from their elders. People tell me and immediately burst into tears. This makes one suspect that our true problem today is not traumas but a severe form of self-indulgence.

To gain a better perspective on your own traumas in life, take a moment now and rate your worst experiences on a scale from 1 to 10, where the most horrible traumas you can think of rank high: being a prisoner in Auschwitz (10), catching the Ebola virus (9), getting taken hostage by terrorists (8). Now, how does your worst trauma rank?

Some readers might have genuinely experienced serious traumas in their lives, and if that is you, in this chapter you will find a practice to help you fully recover from its negative effects. We will also provide you with a method for preventing the debilitating effects of potential future traumas. In addition, for those of you with a distorted sense of trauma in your life, we are also going to make it possible for you to let it go. Because the impact of such lesser traumas can still be debilitating and rob you of your power.

The human mind is simple. It loves uninterrupted routines of comfort and satisfaction, and hates disruptions and defeats. Though it certainly hopes to get more and reach higher, it is more terrified of having less than what it presently has. That's why we strive to design a reality of continuous security and stability, one that leaves no room for bad surprises.

It's the shock of powerlessness when our safe routines are interrupted that makes a situation a trauma. It may be something violent – war, terror, abuse – or it may be something that from the outside might seem trivial – an insult or a dismissive glance. But if it makes you feel powerless, the experience can imprint itself on you forever. When this happens, your mind and body freeze. Have you ever been driving at night when a cat or some wild animal appears in your headlights on the road? It just stops in its tracks. You think it will run, but it is literally frozen in place. The cause of this freeze is an evolutionary response to something so threatening the animal doesn't even try to run away or fight. It just goes rigid. This happens when the animal's best strategy is to play dead and hope the threatening thing will ignore it and go away. It doesn't work well with an approaching car, but the animal's brain is just following its natural response to immense fear.

Our human brain works the same way. The emotional center of our brain, the amygdala, is wired to short-circuit our cerebral cortex in the face of extreme threats with one of three responses, fight, flight or freeze: and freeze is the last resort, the body's survival gambit in the face of total powerlessness. Everything shuts down and we go into a state of shock.

But, unlike the small creature on the road at night, our mind is also present in our moments of extreme powerlessness, even as our sense of normal consciousness blanks out. Our mind does whatever it can to prevent the painful impressions of the moment from fully entering our system. We do this involuntarily to protect ourselves from experiencing horrible things. But, as we have seen throughout this book, whenever we attempt to shield ourselves from experiencing our weakening, it comes at a cost. Resist with all your might a moment of intense weakening, and the impression of that moment will be stamped in you forever. When you resist and freeze you transform a temporary horrible experience into a permanent picture that lives inside of you. It is as if the emotional intensity of the moment fixes in you like a photographic impression. This is the law of suffering: *suffering is your resistance to the weakening and not the weakening itself.* By attempting to avoid pain, you only perpetuate it.

When this happens, situations that in some way remind you of the original trauma can retrigger the fear. As a result, your unconscious mind becomes hyper-alert to situations that might take you back to that feeling, and you will take steps to avoid them at all cost. For example, a childhood dog bite can result in a lifelong fear of all dogs; a bad car accident can result in a fear of travel; an abusive father can result in distrust of all men. The mental, emotional and sensual impressions of that moment take root in you, transforming into inaccurate conceptual generalizations about life. For example that "people are mean," or "you can't trust anyone," or "I have no hope for happiness in this life." Things that people tell you at that time of your trauma may become engraved in your mind so that over time the words come to seem like your own thoughts about yourself. When you resist and freeze, you lose your own presence, so if someone tells you at that moment, "You're worthless!" this is transformed into the internalized thought *I am worthless.*

Children are more exposed to the danger of traumas that stick forever. This is because they have no integrated personality to return to. Their presence is still fluctuating, so any weakening event can enter brutally into their body and mind; anything that people tell them at that time can be absorbed into them easily, blending into their gradually forming personality. But this doesn't mean that significant traumas only happen when you are a child. Whenever your sense of power shatters, you will find yourself passing through the phases of trauma. First, the shock and the freeze. Second, the imprints and inaccurate generalizations. Third, the attempts to retrieve your lost power through replacement, compensation, revenge and concealment – the inefficient process discussed in previous chapters that tries to reconnect the shattered bits so you can feel yourself "in one piece" again.

Our traumas reveal a profound psychological truth. They show us a reality that stays hidden as long as life stretches before us peacefully as series of relaxing habits and routines. Your traumas reveal *your resistance to fully play the game of life*. This is why whenever you are met with intense power loss you use the freeze tactic, even when your life is not immediately threatened. You simply don't want to fully experience your own loss of power. So your mind pretends to be absent, nonexistent, until this unpleasant side of the game goes away. But blocking out your experiences of powerlessness means not accepting life as a whole. That's why such traumas expose your deep, absolute "no" to life.

Participating in the world of power implies the constant possibility of weakening. Your traumas, however, teach you to avoid risks. Yes, some traumas do teach us to avoid unnecessary dangers (don't stick your finger in a light socket; don't tease a bull). However, the negative consequence is that traumas can make you *so* cautious and risk adverse that you start avoiding life's day-to-day power plays:

– "I'd better not strive for success, because if I fail, I'll be humiliated."

– "I shouldn't reveal my attraction to this person, or I will get rejected and hurt."

If your traumas define what you can and cannot do, eventually you will live so minimally, you will be barely alive at all.

Notice in these two examples above that without the speakers' will for *more*, there could be no "trauma" at all. Our principle that *will precedes suffering* works also in the case of traumas. For example, soldiers who get Post Traumatic Stress Disorder (PTSD) go to battle more often than not with great drive to fight, each one for their own reasons. When they meet with a situation of tremendous powerlessness in combat, they are compelled to face the other side of their will. Trauma is a severe shaking of your nature as a walking will. What gets weakened in you is your will and nothing else. Hence, at the moment of trauma you forget what actually happened, what the process of cause and effect really was, and so you are filled with self-pity and victimhood.

The victim-experience springs directly from your own will. You were confidently walking in the path of wish-fulfillment, but then unexpectedly got overpowered by some greater force. Someone else's will was fulfilled at the expense of your weakening. Sometimes, something you considered yours was taken away from you, and in other times, you were prevented from getting something you were hoping to possess.

Try to recall some memory of intense weakening in your life. Reconnect with the humiliation and pain that inevitably followed it. Then honestly ask yourself: "What was the will that I wished to impose on the situation? Could my will have driven me to the situation in the first place? Could it be that my negative experience was nothing but the weakening of this will?" Can you see that the hurt and agony here are only the weakening of your will?

One example from my (Shai) therapeutic work is the story of a fifty-year-old German woman. She was an elegant, reserved and impressive lady, but when she described her traumatic memory, she started sobbing like a little child. She told me that since this traumatic experience occurred, it had marred her entire life! It happened with a woman who was the elegant lady's therapist and spiritual mentor. She had decided to leave this teacher and to develop herself independently. But when she had come to her mentor to say goodbye in one last therapeutic session, the teacher had entered the room and exclaimed: "You? What are *you* doing here again?" She had been stunned by this reaction. In exploring the moment with her, the German woman realized her expectation had been that her teacher would release her with a smile, thus demonstrating once again the "unconditional love" that she, the student, had always demanded. "I wanted her love forever, and I was trying to control it," the lady admitted to me with a smile, now that she was looking at this drama through the eyes of her grown-up self.

But what about all those cases of abuse and coercion? Surely no will drove a person into such painful situations. There are indeed cases of powerlessness that are completely uninvited, from tsunamis to sexual abuse. In such horrific incidents, what got weakened was the person's fixed belief that people should behave in a certain way (supportive and reassuring), and that life should be the way we want it to be (safe and peaceful). Even babies carry such instinctual wishes and demands: they want to be nurtured so that they can grow and get more from life.

It's the person's will for a perfect life and peaceful surroundings that shatters. It's our incredulity that mothers can be unloving, that fathers can be abusive, that life can be cruel and brutal, which lies at the heart of our traumas. Tragically, when naively optimistic beliefs shatter, the person freezes and imprints new generalizations about life. Such generalizations pretend to be "realistic," but in fact they are faulty. For example: "Mothers are cruel and unloving," or "If you go into the water you will drown." Believing these generalizations, born of trauma, keeps the person living in irrational fear that limits their lives.

In the end, all the wills and expectations that precede traumas boil down to one single will: the will to never experience weakening. Indeed, the feeling of weakening during trauma is excruciating. But deep down the trauma that really happened is that you didn't get to live in the world that you wanted. The real world, in the moment of your trauma, was brutal, harsh, and indifferent to your will.

There are two things you can learn from this. First, how to heal a traumatic memory. Second, how to face a potentially traumatic event in such a way as to prevent negative psychic impacts.

To heal a memory that has haunted you for many years you'll need to follow these four steps:

1. *Let go of self-pity:* Refuse to let your past experience of trauma make you a victim. This refusal prevents the formation of the false subconscious around your memory. It is the victim-consciousness that prevents the healing. Remember: you cannot heal the victim; you can only rid yourself of the victim-consciousness and heal your loss of power. Think of it this way: without the feeling of being a victim, what would happen to your memory of the trauma? This is the amazing key: *no victim, no trauma.*

2. *Identify your defeated will:* Connect with your nature as a walking will that only got momentarily weakened in that moment of trauma. Keep in mind that the "traumatic" part of the memory is the humiliation of your power loss when your will was overpowered by others' stronger wills (or simply by hostile nature). Remind yourself that this happened in the past, and that all humans suffer power losses sometimes when they play the game of life. Accept

life's verdict that this time you lost. Now in place of self-pity you can take full responsibility for that event. This does not mean you were to blame for what happened. It means that your will preceded your suffering, and you and you alone are responsible for your will.

3. *Regain your sense of presence:* Your trauma made you freeze. Freezing makes you unaware, as if you are nonexistent. To heal the trauma, you must return to the event with your presence. So first gain a state of presence, through meditation or relaxed breathing or guided visualization (you can use the meditation in Chapter Seventeen to gain presence). Then revisit the memory. Breathe into it. Be there completely and willingly. Agree to the event and heal your resistance to being there. This will enable you to defrost your feelings, to reconnect emotionally, and finally to understand that this was only a temporary state, not a state of being, not the reality of your life. Nourish the memory as you are now experiencing it, as the mature presence and intelligence of the person you have become.

4. *Make it meaningful:* Make the memory part of your conscious and intentional evolution. Find some constructive purpose for it in your life in a context of growth and learning. This is different from compensation. Compensation is about making yourself feel better about the past; this step is about using the experience to make yourself stronger in the future. Remember, you are an active co-creator of your life, even in the most painful of events. You're a curious participant that seeks to learn and develop, and for this to happen, you must take risks. Your trauma might have been a horrible event. Yet you have the power to use it to evolve and become a wiser and more whole person.

Is this asking too much of you, to embrace your worst trauma?

No. Many mature people look back on their lives with gratitude for the worst things that happened to them. For example, I (Shai) think of Nassim Taleb, the Lebanese-American essayist and statistician who spent his adolescent years in the cellar of his house in the north of Lebanon, hiding from the bloody civil war that tore his country apart. Outside his house bombs exploded day and night, while inside he escaped by reading books and contemplating life. He later wrote: "In psychology, people talk about post-traumatic disorder. But very few talk about post-traumatic growth. But actually you need both, and it's even more likely that a trauma will help you than damage you. In fact, the absence of trauma is bad for you... Without the civil war, I would have become a far weaker person."

I (Tim) am friends with a therapist, now in his eighties, who told me that as a child both of his parents abused him physically and emotionally for years. "My one regret is that I never got to thank them for that before they died," he confided to me. "It was their abuse that gave me my drive for deep empathy with people, and that is what made me an effective therapist." And what about the case of the 14-year-old Pakistani girl, riding the bus home from school when a member of the Taliban boarded and shot her, point blank, in the head? Several surgeries saved her life and she recovered, but she still lives under a Taliban death threat for her advocacy of girls' education. The trauma changed Malala Yousafzai forever. It made her stronger. In her 2013 speech to the UN she said:

Dear Friends, on the 9th of October 2012, the Taliban shot me on the left side of my forehead. They shot my friends too. They thought that the bullets would silence us. But they failed. And then, out of that silence came thousands of voices. The terrorists thought that they would change our aims and stop our ambitions but nothing changed in my life except this: Weakness, fear and hopelessness died. Strength, power and courage were born. I am the same Malala. My ambitions are the same. My hopes are the same. My dreams are the same…

In 2014, Malala was awarded the Nobel Peace Prize. Do your traumas rate less than being shot in the head by a terrorist and living under a death threat? Then you can follow Malala's example. Own your trauma and transform your life.

You can also prevent yourself from freezing and losing presence during a traumatic event in real time, before it manages to take root at your being. At a moment of severe weakening, you can employ any of these strategies:

1. *Agree to experience it.* Tell yourself: "This is the game of life; right now I'm on the weaker side, and I intend to experience it fully." Let it forge your being and make you stronger, pass through it as if it were a trial by fire. Remember that accepting traumas means saying "yes" to life. If there is pain, *let the pain flow freely* through your body and mind. Experience this too. Resist the temptation to freeze. Instead, breathe and let it all flow.

2. *Find your will and accept responsibility.* Search for your will that preceded your suffering even while you are suffering. Remember that your will is who you are. Accept its temporary defeat, and remember it will pass. Whoever got the upper hand now, it's just their turn in the game of life. Ask yourself what exactly did they get or are going to get out of this moment? (This will make you accept the game more.) Accepting your defeat will help you resist creating compensations and revenges. Though tempting because they ease the suffering, these mental tricks sap your energy and make you weaker in the long run.

3. *Keep a balanced perspective.* Rate the event from 1 to 10 while it is happening. How bad is it, really? Do you know of

others who are suffering worse than you? If you are at a "5," remind yourself of people in the world living with a "10" in war zones, prisons, or desperate poverty.

4. *Transform your weakening into creative action.* Turn it into an opportunity rather than dwelling in your emotional reactions. The philosopher Friedrich Nietzsche once wrote: *That which does not kill us makes us stronger.* This is only true if you make it so. You can also follow the examples of Nassim Taleb and Malala Yousafzai. Dust yourself off and move forward, facing life and never withdrawing.

Will you find yourself saying…

"Sure, I lived through some traumatic things in my childhood. But I refuse to let them turn me into a victim. No victim, no trauma. It doesn't hold me back."

"I used to think of myself as a victim of trauma. But on a scale of 1–10, what happened to me was really a three. It's ridiculous that I've been letting that experience limit my life. I'm ready to embrace the risk of defeat as the price of saying 'yes' to life."

"What's happening right now is horrible. But I won't freeze, I'll stay present. I can breathe. I can accept that at *this moment* my will is defeated. It's temporary. I can find a way to use even this experience to make me stronger."

Chapter Eleven

Your bursts of aggression

You've heard of Near Death Experiences: someone who drowned, stopped breathing on an operating table, or died in a fatal accident miraculously returns to life. The revived person recounts that while "dead" they were met by angelic beings or a white light that guided them through a review of every moment of their life. They describe this experience as filling them with new hope, purpose and love. Researchers who have studied the thousands of NDEs have found amazing similarities in the many accounts. Our aim here is not metaphysical: people with religious convictions tend to believe these experiences are proof of an afterlife; neuroscientists think they reveal the brain's insistence on making meaning even as it is dying. What we want to focus on is the near universality of the Life Review in NDEs. Putting the question of an afterlife completely aside, the research indicates that at the moment of *your* death, your brain will quite likely go through this Life Review process. What would that be like for you when that happens? Here's what some who went through NDEs said about their experience:

My life appeared before me in the form of what we might consider extremely well-defined holograms, but at tremendous speed. I was astonished that I could understand so much information at such a speed. My comprehension included much more than what I remember happening during each event of my life. I not only re-experienced my own emotions at each moment, but also what others around me had felt. I experienced their thoughts and feelings about me...

When you have a panoramic life review, you literally relive your life, in 360 degrees panorama. You see everything that's ever happened.

You even see how many leaves were on the tree when you were six-years-old playing in the dirt in the front yard. You literally relive it. Next you watch your life from a second person's point of view... You will feel what it feels like to be that person and you will feel the direct results of your interaction between you and that person.

As a child she made fun of a scrawny, malnourished asthmatic kid who eventually died from a cerebral aneurysm. The kid once wrote a love letter to her which she rejected. In her life review, she experienced his pain of being rejected...

(For more, see:

http://www.near-death.com/experiences/research24.html #a04)

Imagine what it would be like to re-experience every act of aggression you committed in your life, not just seeing all the details clearly, but fully and completely feeling the emotions of every person you have hurt. Remember, the beings of light are witness to your Life Review. They see it all. The curtain of secrecy has been removed, so everything is revealed and nothing can be denied. Do you cringe even at the thought of this? Or do you say, "Well, that's not so bad. Sure, I might have hurt a few people, but only when I had no choice, only in self-defense..." Can you recognize this voice speaking to you as your self-image, desperate to preserve your sense that you are a "good" person?

The hard work of this chapter is to face your acts of aggression, to own them, to feel those moments totally and honestly. You don't have to wait for your NDE. You can go through this experience now. Probably you are thinking, "Why on earth would I want to do *that?*" You want to keep your acts of aggression secret, even to yourself. The answer is that acts of aggression – more specifically, the *bursts* of aggression that seem to erupt from you with great forcefulness – constrict your life, and actually deny you true inner power. The purpose of this chapter is not to simply re-experience such moments, but to transform yourself through this practice in five specific ways (which we will explain in detail at the end of the chapter) that will bring more freedom, power and love into your life.

Most people find it hard to see raw aggression in themselves, but very easy to locate in others: "Yes, I know all about it – my husband suffers from this!" or "Do you mean things like what my father did to me when I was a child?" Everything we have learnt until now – the mask of concealment and the self-image, the victim-consciousness, the false subconscious and the habit of diversion – gathers to deny this part of your reality. There are of course the obvious extremes of aggression in which you might have not participated: sexual abuse, physical violence, or emotional terror. However, there are also subtler expressions of aggression: silent manipulations to get something, lies to hurt someone, deliberately turning a blind eye to the suffering of others, sending small but deliberate signals of loathing, hatred, scorn and spite capable of cutting someone right to the heart. To this we can add internal acts of aggression: death wishes, megalomaniac hallucinations in which everyone is under our dominion, sadistic fantasies, and any wish to get something without caring about others' feelings.

No one is free from these bursts of aggression, so the journey you are going to take in this next practice will bring you into territory shared by all humanity. Yet you will experience it as a place totally unique to you, buried in the darkness of your psyche. We promise you, if you open that door following our instructions, you will never be afraid of this place again.

As a first step you need to find a quiet place alone where you won't be disturbed for about an hour. Bring a pen and paper. Sit quietly with yourself, and invite the recollections of your bursts of aggression, subtle and blatant, to surface. Most likely you will find it easy to come up with at least two or three. If you think that you have drawn a blank, that there is nothing there, that you have always been the innocent victim surrounded by real aggressors, please consider that a door might still be locked to you. This barrier is a diversion of your false subconscious. Let go of your identification with yourself as a victim and invite in other memories and start again.

Write down your memories of ten different bursts of aggression. After the first few you may face this barrier, as if there are no more. As you persevere you'll get a chain of memories appearing as if from nowhere. Some of these may be tough to acknowledge, perhaps incidents known only to you and your victims. Ignore the interpretation you gave these events in the past that justified your behavior in order for you to live with it. Ignore the diversions that shift the blame for the aggression to another person, or to the circumstances forced on you, or to your past traumas that "drove you" to this outburst. Forget the excuses, and focus on the event.

Keep going until you have collected ten memories of aggression and you have written them down. Just writing a key word, a person's name or the location will do. Now, start at the top of the list and work your way down. Look at each event closely. Don't turn your head away. They are part of your past, of yourself. Imagine this as part of your Life Review displayed on a hologram, or movie projector, and you can see each and every vivid detail. It will be like reliving the event in slow motion, but this time, unlike when it happened, it will be with your eyes fully open. You will be getting a complete picture of yourself. You won't distort, won't deny. It is also an important feature of the Life Review that the celestial beings who witness it with you do not judge. It is crucial in this exercise that you adopt this non-judging perspective too. See everything clearly, but set your moral mask aside. This is not about being a good or bad person. It is about facing your reality and *feeling it fully*.

When I (Tim) went through this exercise, I found it intensely painful, like ripping a scab off a wound, ten times. I noticed myself struggling with feelings of depression (literally striving to depress my awareness). I fell asleep in the middle of the exercise, sitting in a chair in the middle of the afternoon! I finally woke up and continued to the end. It was hard for me to fend of my false subconscious telling me I had my reasons, that it couldn't be helped, and to keep my awareness on the scenes as they fully and vividly unfolded.

Look at such moments as they actually were: eruptions of your will, uncensored expressions of your primordial wish. These are the times when your power-wish could no longer tolerate the usual restraints of culture and morality. It wanted to get what it wanted, and just got tired of pretending to be nice. Ah, all those endless compromises we make with the reality of billions of other wills! What polite concealment! In your bursts of aggression everything you secretly yearned to do but didn't dare finally escaped your control. For that brief moment you threw aside the mask and took what you wanted. For once the predator didn't need to use a knife and fork to enjoy the prey.

Pay attention to your own internal state as you recollect each of your ten events. To allow a burst of aggression, you need to intensely harden your being so that you feel nothing. It's similar to the freeze in trauma, only here you lock the centers of feeling to prevent the flow of emotions for other reasons: you need to bring yourself to a state of pure wanting, wanting that only wishes to impose itself on its surroundings and completely take over. You're like a soldier in combat that must shut down all emotions if he wants to focus on conquering the target. A soldier cannot afford to break down and cry at every horrifying and bloody sight around him. So you need to perceive the other that shrinks in power beside you coldly and as if from a great distance in order to turn them into mere objects and use them.

Immediately after each burst of aggression, what happened? Your culture returned to you. You needed to somehow explain to yourself and the shocked others what took place. We tend to do this in three ways that actually make us weaker. First, it's very common for people to say after such bursts: "Something came over me," or "I don't know what possessed me at that time." Why does this happen? Your self-image maintains that you're a good person. So to recognize such raw aggression as part of who you are is unbearable. You had to be overcome by some external force – just like in trauma. In other words, to let this happen you had to be weak. Second, in the moments after an act of aggression, we often condemn ourselves. Horrified by what we have just done, we may make a vow to abstain from *any* use of our power, as if that will keep the world safe from future abuse at our hands. This vow starves our will from any outward expression, and that makes us weak. Third, we sometimes justify what we have done with a self-defense argument, *the aggression of the weak*: "They pushed me to that," we say, or "I had no choice but to defend myself!" In both condemnation and justification it's always some external factor we blame for making us behave aggressively. In so doing we deny our agency and our responsibility for our acts.

The truth is, not only did you commit your acts of aggression, you were never more present. In the midst of such an outburst you are the most "you" that can ever be: raw and untamed will, a will that always cultivated the fantasy of immoral, unrestrained self-expression. Just like a river pressing on a dam for too long, when the water rises high enough, the dam will burst, violently and destructively.

I (Shai) once led a workshop in Germany on true inner power in which I asked the participants to bring up some memory in which they felt they possessed true inner power. I was taken by surprise when more responded by relating their bursts of aggression. They told me that in such events they felt they were finally their real selves, being in their full power. They didn't find it disturbing at all that this happened at the expense of another, because, they argued, they were acting in self-defense. They emphasized only their feelings of self-expansion and cathartic release. But if you dare to take a penetrating look into the reality of this kind of eruption, you'll see something else that is unsettling.

Bursts of aggression are the flip side of traumas. While in traumas your whole being is reduced into a state of minimal power-experience, so that sometimes the only power left is your mere survival, in bursts of aggression your power overflows to such an extent that it becomes forceful and coercive. You grow in power at the expense of others' weakening, and often unashamedly usurp their power. It's like being so intoxicated by the fulfillment of your will that you become indifferent to the damage you cause others. In some cases, you may even sadistically enjoy watching them suffer. Just like in trauma, during bursts of aggression you retreat to a state of minimal awareness of your surroundings. Only here this constriction of awareness has a different purpose: not seeing anything other than your object of desire or hatred. Your being becomes fully concentrated, not recognizing anymore real faces and real victims, just the "thing" that you want or the "obstacle" you need to remove.

That's why most bursts of aggression have something to do with a clash between your will and the opposing will of another.

In such instances you felt that the only way for you to get what you wanted was to force it with all your might. Of course, if you put a camera on at those moments to be your silent witness of the situation, you would likely feel terrible: from the outside you look like a crazy person, a grotesque and trance-like being who has lost all self-control in the effort to fully control another person. When the tables turn against you, and others burst aggressively at you, these situations usually become your traumas. Then you experience what it is like to be treated as an empty husk, a *thing* for the will-fulfillment of another. You become a faceless object, and this, as you well recall, is a devastating and humiliating experience. When you do that to another person in your burst of aggression, something constricts in you, hardens, and freezes. As long as this hardness stays in you, you will be blocked from the full flowing freedom life has to offer you.

So, now that you have fully and honestly faced the memories of your aggression in the first part of this practice, how can you transform them into energy you can use to develop inner power? Truthfully, you'll only understand this fully after you manage to transform one memory. There are five steps to this part of the practice. Some of them are new applications of techniques you already learned in previous chapters. Each step has its own benefit along the way:

1. *Accept ownership of your aggression.* This will free you from the eternal victim. When you embrace your bursts of aggression as part of your true self, you challenge the self-image of the eternal victim – an image that keeps you in a state of minimal power. When you accept you're not just a defenseless pure soul, but someone capable of aggression – of evil, if you like – then you can claim the energy of that evil as your own. So the first step you need to take is giving up your story that this was not "you" who did this

horrible thing. Then give up the condemnation or justification that separates you from your outbursts. Instead, take responsibility and ownership: "This was not some form of demon possession. This was *me* expressing my primordial wishes in an unfiltered way. Yes, I am this predator." If you're capable of such forcefulness, this means you are already in possession of great power.

2. *Locate your primordial wish behind each burst of aggression.* Recognize your primordial wish as the cause of your aggression. This makes you conscious of your strong will that wishes to create reality in its own image. For each of your ten memories, turn them over, as you learned to do in Chapter Two with episodes of frustration. Expose the wish behind each outburst. Ask yourself: what was my unrestrained wish in that event? Then, as you learned to do at the end of Chapter Three, turn these wishes into a useful energy through the practice offered there.

3. *Transform the energy of each memory into pure power.* Bursts of aggression can be transformed from force into pure power and pure presence. This step is particularly significant for those who suffer from a sense of powerlessness. Working with such memories makes the clenched fist inside of you loosen its grip, releasing a new flow of energy into your body and mind. Just close your eyes again and relive one burst of aggression in great detail, reconnecting with the feelings, sensations and perceptions that you had at that time. Pay special attention to the intense and heated force that came through you. When you feel you have gathered enough of this force, drop the memory and remain only with this tremendous, vibrating energy. Feel it in the present moment. Then turn it inwards: let it fill your entire body and being, breathe into it and let it flow from head to toe, like molten lava or wind from a blast furnace making it a gushing flow of presence. As you feel it flow,

acknowledge that this great power already exists within you. You are literally transforming the memory of your "evil" back into the raw energy of will. Now you can use this energy for whatever you like. Whenever you need inner strength, you can come back to this exercise to charge yourself up. For example, whenever you're on your way to confront a challenge in your life that demands great inner strength.

4. *Grow in love.* Strange as it seems, your ugliest moments of cold-hearted aggression can help you to develop empathy and love. When you recall these memories, you can see how your heart was empty and shut at the time. Expanding your awareness of the pain that you caused others can reawaken the emotional system that had closed down. In this way, your bursts of aggression can lead you to conscious awareness of the other's existence in a profound way. Your primordial wish cares about no one but itself. As long as your will is content and you are wearing the mask of goodness, you are never deeply aware of other people. The unique clash of wills that leads to a burst of aggression opens a gateway for you to become fully conscious of the reality of the other. When you truly see, you will no longer wish to appropriate and objectify someone else. You'll feel that you want to give the other an equal opportunity to express their own power. This awakens something awesome into your life: the growth of goodness out of your badness; the growth of love out of violence. In this way, bursts of aggression can teach you compassion beyond ordinary morality.

To practice the growth of love, bring up one of your ten memories of aggression and relive it just like you did in step number 3, above. This time don't focus on the force that erupted from within you. Instead, focus on your victims. Become more and more conscious of them: look at them closely, at their sorrowful face, feel their distress and weakness, allow the feelings that exist in you today to become present in that event. Observe the tyrant that you were in that moment through the victim's perspective. What do you see when looking at yourself through their eyes? Expand your attention more and more. You can expect it to hurt as your emotions come to life and you feel what they felt. But if you pass through the hurt, it will lead you eventually to include both your being and the other's in the full reality of the moment. Keep in mind, this is not about asking forgiveness or feeling remorseful. You are *learning to experience love and compassion beyond morality.* The point is shifting beyond the solitary, egoistical view of life, and welcoming into your world the reality of the other person and their will. To complete the practice after your meditation is finished, allow someone to fulfill their will at the expense of your will sometime soon. Do it out of the recognition of the existence of other wills beside your own.

5. *Rid yourself of negative charges and imprints.* Everyone easily accepts that their traumas can cause psychological and physical distress, but they don't think this way about their aggressions. Like traumas, bursts of aggression also create deep-seated imprints and patterns of behavior that can accumulate as negative charges and imprints within your mind and body. So if you're seeking therapy to remove negative charges and imprints, tell your therapist also about the aggressive parts of your past and suggest focusing on these events as well as the traumas.

Having completed the practice of this chapter, you will be much more conscious of what is happening to you next time you experience a clash of wills with another, and feel the inner bubbling of energy that signals an imminent burst of aggression. You can also use the technique from Chapter Ten for dealing with trauma to prevent your aggressive impulses from boiling over: First, rate the severity of the situation between 1 to 10, with 10 as the most justified aggression. For example, are you fending off someone who is trying to kill you? That would be a "10." Is someone you love being rude to you? Honestly, how bad is it? This technique will give you distance and perspective. Second, when you feel the crazy dictator arising inside of you, resist the tendency to erase the reality of the person you are clashing with. Instead, look directly into their eyes and acknowledge they are *here*. As soon as you realize the full reality of the other, be thankful for this moment of your expanded presence. This can flip the potential for violence completely on its head. You might find yourself suddenly filled with love and empathy for the other person. Or you might simply start to laugh.

Will you find yourself saying…

"I know I've hurt some people in my life. I take responsibility for my outbursts of aggression. I don't blame anyone else, and I'm certainly no victim. But I don't condemn myself either. What I learned from my past outbursts is that I've got tremendous power. I want to channel that power consciously from now on, not let it explode out of control."

"Wow, I'm having such an aggressive power fantasy right now, imagining what I would like to do to that hateful person. What would happen if I looked in their eyes and saw their full humanity? How would that change the scene?"

"You make me so *angry*, insulting me like that in front of my friends… and it's, oh, well, on a scale of justified aggression from one to ten, I guess it's about a… two." (Laughs.)

Chapter Twelve

Accepting life's contract

There is one thing that I (Shai) learned after working for the past fifteen years with many hundreds of people who walk in the path of self-awareness: so many people today experience themselves as utterly fragile and vulnerable. Anything someone says to them that feels a bit insulting or annoying, any "wrong" reaction on their partner's part, any slight change or moderate upheaval in their life – they experience it *so* intensely. In fact it often shakes them to the root of their being. But why is that so? In Chapter Nine we discussed how the liberal humanistic approach puts the sanctity of the individual at the center of the world. So as a culture we've become obsessed with fixing the psychological effects of the individual's traumas and victimhood. The significance of every feeling is magnified and analyzed. You've been educated all your life as if the most crucial and important question is: "How do I feel right now?" Ironically, this weakens you.

However, there's an even deeper reason. It seems that with the ease and convenience of life in our modern Western culture we have lost the resilience and sturdiness we had in earlier ages. When a living creature is busy fighting against intense forces in order to survive, it often develops a better "immune system," emotionally and mentally. In the 21st century, we are hardly fighting at all. You, the reader of this book, have probably never faced an acute struggle for your very survival (barring accident or disease). The security and quality of your life is astonishing compared with the demanding conditions of earlier times. That's why I (Shai) have come to realize that in the more advanced and refined cultures of Europe, inner weakness is actually increasing!

Let's return for a moment to Nassim Taleb, the thinker we

quoted in Chapter Ten on the positive value of our traumas. In his book *Antifragile* he asserts that humans in the 21st century have created for themselves a life resembling that of a tourist on a carefully organized tour. In this artificial form of life people try to completely remove any type of discomfort. On top of that, they then try to remove even the slightest uncertainty, fluctuation, randomness or pressure. Instead of benefiting from the unpredictable nature of reality, we strive to assume full control over it. The irony, claims Taleb, is that all this effort to turn the world into a predictable and comfortable place causes us to be more fragile, more sensitive to the turbulences of life. We see this in the doctor who rushes to prescribe a patient unnecessary medication that overrides the body's natural healing abilities, and in the overprotective parent who drives the children to playdates and music lessons and never lets them go anywhere unescorted. As a species, writes Taleb, we only weaken our health, politics, economics and education by suppressing randomness and instability. His solution: to upend this tendency and stop trying to impose order on reality. Accepting life's unpredictable dynamics, he declares, can help us benefit from uncertainty and disorder.

This is the great confusion we're all caught in: we're convinced that if we assumed full control over reality and made of our life a small island of false stability we would achieve more power. But it's this false stability that weakens us, because we are losing our natural immunity. You're more resilient when you need to struggle with inconvenience and uncertainty. Just as a child's immune system becomes stronger when challenged by the normal dust and dirt of a home, and weaker when the child is kept in a too-sterile environment, so too does the psyche weaken when not exposed to intense pressures from time to time. Such a person becomes so weak that almost any disturbance can shake and break them.

Sometimes to get more stability and confidence people turn to spiritual practices, like meditation. But from my (Shai) experience as a teacher of inner transformation, these practices are often self-defeating: they seem to remove the practitioners' vital defenses and filters. People become more "relaxed" and "accepting," but this state works best in the protected environment of the workshop or retreat. In the real world, these people usually discover that their vital protections have been severely damaged, and so they cannot truly function and get fully involved. They have become too soft and delicate to live in the world. I (Tim) saw a vivid example of this during the months I lived in a Buddhist monastery in the jungles of eastern Thailand. The monks seldom went into the nearby town, and when they had to go (for example, to acquire needed supplies) they would often come back overwhelmed and exhausted from the sensory overstimulation. "All that *samsara!*" I would hear them complain. I wondered what was the value of a spiritual practice that made it too hard for a person to go shopping.

That's why the process you're going through while reading this book and practicing these exercises is so important. You need power. Power is vital to your mental and emotional health, and to your sense of self-wholeness. You also need will, a solid will, to fully participate in life. With inner power and solid will you can take part in the power plays without needing to withdraw to some dark and safe corner of your interior world.

So what is the starting point for creating true inner power? You must *accept life's contract*. This is the contract you unconsciously signed immediately after your birth. You wrote, "Yes!" in response to the question: "Would you agree to take an active part in the world of power?" In other words, you agreed to live. Perhaps you didn't imagine back then what this world of power would actually look like. That's why you need to sign the contract again, consciously this time, as an adult. Otherwise, you'll be forever evading the reality of the world; any sense of inner power you'll gain along the way will most probably be the sweet caress of self-deluded compensation.

"Fine," you might say, "but this contract sounds too vague. I want to know what it actually means before I sign it!" The basic terms are what you have been learning about in this book: that life is a struggle for power and a constant effort to avoid weakness. It means that you say "yes" to life as a battlefield of wills which forever strive to overpower each other in order to get expressed and fulfilled. But wait – when we describe it in this way, it makes it sound like there are two parties to the contract, you and "life." So here's the great enlightenment: *you're an inseparable part of this world, made of exactly the same substance as every other bit of it.* This substance is hard, forged by billions of years of violent natural evolution: in space, the stars, and here on earth. You're much tougher than you're willing to admit. Deep down, beneath the "good person" of the self-image, you're just like anyone else. You seek your own power and you are fascinated by this game – this game that is nothing but energy coursing through the universe and through your veins. Perhaps you feel too weak to participate, and for that you hate this game, but that's a different problem. When you understand where you are (in a battlefield) and who you are (an ardent player in this game), you can no longer resist it or separate yourself from it. That will be the end of your self-image as a fragile creature constantly shocked by all the violence around you. The fact that you're disinclined to participate in blatant acts of force and violence doesn't mean you're made of a different substance. It only means your struggle is more refined.

When you experience yourself as fragile, what you really mean to say is: "I'm not as powerful as others, as I'd like to be." When you exclaim in moments of desperation, "I hate this world!" what you really feel is: "I'm frustrated by the power plays; I feel so unbearably weak and I'm not willing to face my defeat." What you really hate when you hate the world is this danger of your weakening, the state of being unable to fulfill your power. It's just what Peter Belmi, a researcher from the Stanford Graduate School of Business, describes in his research on beauty and social status: "When we think we're on the top, we tend to believe that hierarchies are a good thing. When we think we're in the bottom, we tend to believe in equality." We like the world as long as we're the ones sitting on top of it.

If you hate the world, you probably have attempted to evade life's contract, perhaps by turning your inner world into a "home" that shelters you from feelings of weakness. Some harbor the longing to "return to the womb," "go to heaven," or enter some state of mind and body that seems to resemble it. Others long for someone, a romantic partner or a guru, who will accept them unconditionally and make them feel they have one spot in which they're not expected to fight for their place. The quest for these types of havens is only a by-product of the difficulties one faces on the way to achieving power in the world. You only want to escape when it doesn't work or when you're afraid it won't work.

The weaker you feel, the greater your longing for an escape to an inner fantasy world. Perhaps that's understandable. If life on earth were an amusement park ride, it would probably come with a sign that reads: "Warning! Not recommended for the faint-hearted!" But even if you're escaping in your mind, you're still here and the contract still awaits your signature. No matter how much you fantasize about alternative realities, you cannot really escape, and when you try to escape in your mind, this weakens you dramatically. Face it: this is a tough place, yet there's no other place. Let go of your inner sanctuary and step in. When you step in, declare: "I'm made of the same stuff as the so-called external world. I'm hard too, and that makes me perfectly capable of being fully present. Right *here* is where I belong."

By accepting the life's contract consciously, you'll need to add to it a few new sections, just to be completely clear what you are committing yourself to:

1. *I agree to want.* True, everyone wants at least to some degree, but very few want powerfully and confidently. Most of us want with great hesitation and caution, quickly preparing alternatives and compensations. This is because you already know very well the pain involved in a possible defeat. You educate yourself not to want too strongly to avoid this pain. With this strategy you refrain from many of your passions, narrow down your possibilities in life and only end up weaker.

2. *I agree to experience weakness.* This is the flip side of agreeing to want. As we saw from the chapter on compensations, accepting your moments of weakness as part of the game actually empowers you. As long as you're terrified of weakening, you're not truly alive: you become alert and cautious and avoid everything that signals danger. Power can only be achieved when one accepts the risk of weakening and the possibility of suffering. In fact, the more you want power, the more willingly you will risk being exposed to this danger. When you agree to weakening, you don't need to waste extra energy in fighting it. In fact if you're unafraid of such moments, there is no real weakening beyond the moment. Unexpectedly, this makes you much stronger, capable of creatively responding and quickly moving on.

3. *I agree to experience harsh and tough conditions.* If you want to develop and grow, you'll need some degree of friction with reality. Difficult situations (physically and emotionally), harsh environments, pressure, deprivations, all these things make you tougher. They are the forge in which you can create an unbreakable self. Agree to the possibility of trauma. This doesn't mean that you should endanger yourself, but that if you find yourself in a

traumatic situation, use it for growth, as outlined in Chapter Ten. Make friends with your problems. They make you strong and they force you to be present in order to deal with them. So ignore the voice in your head that wishes your problems would all disappear. Even bad news, negative messages, unfair criticisms, betrayals and major disappointments can empower you to learn, to regroup, and develop resilience. Remind yourself: *That which doesn't kill me, makes me stronger.*

4. *I agree to get my hands dirty.* Many people feel that to get deeply involved in this world of power you must be egoistical and bad. You can't remain good and uncorrupted and at the same time step fully into the power plays; at least some degree of cunning and manipulation is necessary if you want to "swim with the sharks." So it's better to do very little and stay clean. But that's the cop-out of people who have only watched from the sidelines.

To get off the sidelines and into the game you have to be prepared to deal with impure motives. When people learn about their hidden motives – replacement, compensation, revenge and concealment – they often say: "If all my actions are tainted by these lower impulses, I'd rather refrain from any action until all my motives are pure." But is it wise to stop everything you're doing and withdraw into a state of intense contemplation until perfection is reached? No. You can always find traces of psychological impurities in any of your actions. Though it's good to understand why you're doing what you're doing, it's even better to keep acting while you gradually learn to purify your motives. This allows you to keep the flow of creative activity in your life, even if, for example, you know that you're being driven by an incessant revenge-wish.

The same principle applies when it comes to making mistakes. Everyone makes mistakes. To err is human. Yet we fear them. We try to shift the blame, deny our responsibility, and sometimes fight hard to convince others we were right, even when we know we were mistaken. This is because it's not really the mistakes one fears, only the weakening that might follow – loss of prestige, ridicule, a blow to one's self-image. So agree to the weakening caused by your mistakes, and then you won't have to put your life on hold until you're perfect. Now you can make mistakes and learn from them instead of fearing them. Remember: where there is action, there is energy, and only where there is energy is there the possibility of change and growth.

5. *I agree to be less powerful than many others.* Imagine the world of power as a pyramid: its narrow, sharp top can accommodate very few, while its base is generous and accommodates most of us. So comparing your powers with others' powers will not make you happy. Genuine self-acceptance is accepting the degree of power with which you came into the world, and using what you've got to reach your maximum potential: the best possible version of yourself. When you contemplate your potential, be careful not to think of it as what you would wish to become. Our potential is usually much closer to our actual abilities than one might think. So instead of asking, "How can I attain great powers in this lifetime?" ask this far more incisive question: "How can I maximize the fulfillment of the best parts of me?"

6. *I agree to be humble.* To be humble means to be a realist. It means to realize you are not the center of the universe. This means to accept you won't get everything you want in life, and that to get what you want will take effort. This may not come easily to those of us who grew up pampered and self-indulgent in our culture of comfort and convenience. People want to be always who they really are, to be unconditionally accepted, to be heard all the time and to

never suffer from the need to compromise. They don't "feel like" living in a world of forced replacements and compromise with many other billions of wills. When they do compromise, they whine bitterly about it. When their primordial wish is blocked, they respond with anger or depression, as if they expect the rest of the world will always surrender to the will of their inner dictator. They behave like spoiled children who have been overindulged by their parents. One typical example of this is men who want to enjoy the benefits of monogamous relationship while wishing to be allowed to have sex with anyone they want. Another example is college students who expect their ideal job awaits them upon graduation, and they will accept nothing less.

To agree to be a realist in life means ceasing your violent emotional struggle with reality when it does not immediately give you what you think you deserve. Work hard to earn your place in the world. Learn to compromise with others. Drop the expectation that life owes you anything. That's not in the contract! When you realize your spoiled inner child is making unrealistic demands on life, gently tell yourself to wake up. Then accept your humble place as one of eight billion people on the planet.

7. *I agree to see the beauty of the game.* You might be tempted to think that the struggles of life are always harsh and ugly. Nothing could be further from the truth. The power plays of nature and humanity have produced great beauty. Through evolution, competition between and within species gives rise to an astounding diversity of forms: the peacock's tail, the dolphin's grace, the petals of a rose. Generation after generation each living thing is continuously shaped into something new by life's constant power struggles. Our species is no exception, although our consciousness has opened humanity to whole new arenas

for power plays. For example, science and the arts thrive through competition as they explore new ways to engage reality. Even our evil – war, dictatorships, and enslavement – has released tremendous energy into the world as other forces rise to overcome it. Indeed, power plays maintain a vital balance both in culture and in nature. No one species takes over the whole planet (not even us); eventually the strongest dictators weaken and must accommodate the wills of others. Finally, even the suffering and struggle of an individual has the potential to spur his or her mental and spiritual evolution. This dynamic, interior process of transformation, which lies at the heart of this book, creates something magnificent within a person. So embrace life's struggle as the foundation of life's beauty.

8. *I agree to have this world as my home.* The final clause of your agreement invites you to forge a new alliance with life in the world. Many people cultivate the wish to retire – and not just from the rat race. They seek to attain some kind of enduring state of peace and restfulness. This wish is a natural outcome of exhaustion from their many defeats and frustrations in the ceaseless power plays of life. In some people this desire develops into various imaginative escape fantasies. Others work diligently and practically to finance their early retirement so they can move away to a golfing community or beach house. Those with a spiritual or religious bent are more likely to yearn for heaven or nirvana. Even films often end "happily ever after" with the main characters settling into a quiet and peaceful family life at the end of their struggles and adventures.

But if you can only get through life by longing for some other place you would rather be, this means you're only partly here. To be fully engaged in the here and now, you need to start thinking of planet earth as your true home, as your *only* home. Imagine what it is like to believe in reincarnation in which you are reborn forever and ever, for all eternity, without the possibility of escape. Can you embrace such a vision? Try saying this out loud: "Yes, I agree to incarnate forever as a human, and over and over again to face the difficulties and harshness of this world. I will never seek to escape, not even in my mind. I whole-heartedly commit to this endless power struggle of life, even if that means eternal restlessness and agitation. I leave behind my unrealistic primordial wish for a comfortable and pleasant life, a life in which I always get whatever I want. I agree to this life just as it is, forever and ever." Now, can you live just this one present lifetime with this same commitment? This way of thinking will give you a completely different kind of peace of mind.

These, in sum, are the eight principles of your conscious contract with life. Don't rush to accept this contract too swiftly. Give the terms time to sink in. If and when you agree, your practice for this chapter is simple: sign the contract below.

My Conscious Contract with Life

1. I agree to want.

2. I agree to experience weakness.

3. I agree to experience harsh and tough conditions.

4. I agree to get my hands dirty.

5. I agree to be less powerful than many others.

6. I agree to be humble.

7. I agree to see the beauty of the game.

8. I agree to have this world as my home.

Signed:

Date:

Having signed Life's Contract, will you find yourself saying...

"Everybody is being so hard on me at work. It's so unfair. But wait, I signed *Life's Contract*. I agreed to experience harsh conditions. I'd better toughen up."

"Why can't people just give me what I want? It's so aggravating they don't just do it my way. But wait, I signed *Life's Contract*, I agreed life doesn't owe me anything. I'm one of eight billion. I agreed to be humble."

"I hate my life right now. I just want to get away from it all and live on a deserted island. Sometimes, I even think it would be a relief to be dead. But wait, I signed *Life's Contract*. I agreed to make this world my home forever. I've got to get my head back in the game."

Chapter Thirteen

One will to rule them all

"What do you want out of life?"

I (Shai) asked this question of a 36-year-old woman who had come to see me for a private session. She was an impressive woman, with a very active lifestyle. She had completed at least a dozen different programs in alternative medicine and had a thriving practice as a therapist. But when I asked her what she wanted to achieve in our session, she said she didn't really know. So I asked the big question, "What do you want out of life?" She responded with a shrug and muttered confused, "It's like I no longer want anything from life." I didn't think she was lying to me, but I didn't believe her, either.

Of course it is the entire premise of this book that people *want*. You are a walking will and so long as you are alive there is no such thing as "not wanting." Even a monk meditating in a cave is there because he wants self-mastery and enlightenment. So, keeping in mind the principle that *will precedes suffering*, I asked the young therapist in my office to describe her emotional pains and sorrows. She could do this easily. From there it was possible to ask her to look beneath her suffering, to identify what wills of hers got frustrated in her life, and thus to help her uncover what she really wanted. The question, though, is how did this accomplished young woman end up with such strong yet empty feelings of "not wanting" in the first place?

What I (Shai) have learned in my years as a therapist is that when people say they don't know what they want, this really means they feel unable to *fulfill* their wants. When you say you want nothing, or that you don't know what you want, this means a certain inner process has taken place within you that has twisted your perception. You are partly aware of your will, yet you want to keep it hidden from yourself. This feeling of confusion or of "not wanting" is the end result of this inner dynamic. Untwisting this perception in yourself in order to *give you full access to what you really want* is the purpose of this chapter.

If you look inside your mind you will find a constant battle is taking place. Opposing forces compete with each other, each one striving to get your attention and preference. Sometimes impulse wins the battle against routine: you rebel and take a day off work. Sometimes fear overpowers the urge to take a risk: you decide to play it safe and just do what is expected of you. Every time a different force surfaces, if you give it more attention than other forces – if you claim that force as "mine" – it will take over. If you are able to focus on just one force and give little attention to other forces, this gives you enough willpower to get what you want the most. For example, let's say you want to write a book. To do so, you have to focus on that urge to write and pay much less attention to competing urges. If you can keep your focus, in the end you will have a book.

But what are all these forces that compete inside you? How can you wisely choose between them? On the face of it you just feel a struggle between different emotions and thoughts: fears, desires, ambitions, hopes, past disappointments and so on, each one pulling you in a different direction. This makes it a very complex and complicated picture. But what if we told you that it's all really a struggle between different wills?

Let's go back to the example of writing a book. Imagine yourself as an aspiring author who has only one ambition, to write from your creative urge. But then other wants come along, so that the original will becomes divided and entangled. You begin to imagine those first pages will turn into a bestseller, a work of genius admired by many. Fame and fortune will surely follow and you discover that you keenly desire that, too. Then fear of failure strikes: "I want to be considered a genius, but what if I can't live up to my ideal of myself? What if this book exposes my lack of talent?" Next fear of rejection hits. What if no publisher wants to publish the manuscript? Now you feel a sudden, powerful desire to take a break. An internal voice urges, "You know, I really feel like meeting up with my friends for a coffee." This transforms into a new conviction: "After all, I can't spend my life working at the computer; I deserve to take a break and enjoy myself, too..."

Whenever you want more than one thing, and are unwilling to forgo any of your many wills, you can get trapped in this kind of paralyzing inner struggle. It's a common human experience, yet you would think we would know better. How could we hope to fulfill all our wills at once, especially when they contradict each other? Our struggle is like a cliché: We want to have our cake and eat it too. Of course the reason this is such a near universal experience is because it comes from a common source: our primordial wish, our deep desire to have it all. How wonderful it could be to have an easy and carefree life, writing brilliant books that publishers want to publish, both crowd-pleasers and critically acclaimed, and yet the writing flows effortlessly and with great joy...

Let's imagine for a moment a state in which all that exists within you is your primordial wish: unashamed, fully declared, and never contradicted by any other will. In such a godlike state you'll have only one will, and so you won't feel any inner conflict. This is quite similar to the psychic state of very young children. But when a toddler's amazingly simple mind reaches a certain level of development, he or she recognizes the existence of other minds and other wills. That is the beginning of the temper tantrums of "the terrible twos." As each of us grew through this phase, we started developing conflicting wills. We became aware of the power-relations in the world and a culture that forced us to accept morality and compromise. We developed the will to conform and to attain social approval. Conscious of our degree of authentic power compared to others, and fearful of the danger of weakening, we also developed replacement-wills as safe alternatives (we will go into these in more detail below).

Take for example the battle between selfishness and selflessness. Your primordial wish would like to selfishly pursue your desires and ambitions while your social image would like to prove that you're selfless and loving. Which will do you think most often prevails, selfish or selfless? Most often selflessness wins. No wonder: it's the one that gets more support from society and family. Selfless wills are also safer. A selfish will provokes the danger of weakening in the event of loss. This is a danger most people seek to avoid.

To return to our starting point: the real problem is not that we don't want, or that we have no energy to want strongly. Actually we have more *wanting energy* than we can possibly imagine. A fireball of passion and lust burns in each of us. What nullifies the force of this great energy of wanting is that it has split and splintered over time into contradictory wills that cancel each other out. It's like noise-cancelling headphones: they produce sound waves that are the exact opposite of the noise surrounding the wearer; when perfectly opposing sound waves intersect, they flatten out and the result is total silence.

You can begin to distinguish the conflicting wills in your life by trying this quick thought experiment:

Think of something in your life that gives you the feeling, "I don't know what I want." Now replace that thought with the new thought: "I want to get a few things here that contradict each other at the same time." Examine whether this better fits the reality inside you. When you want different things at the same time, you end up feeling that you want nothing.

There's a deeper layer to this predicament. When you look into the source of this struggle between your wills, you'll realize it's happening because *you are afraid to want your real and original will.* Most of the conflicting wills that appear in you are just replacement-wills. They offer you alternative powers to the one true power you're striving to gain. Replacement-wills are the powers that your mind reserves just in case your true will gets thwarted or rejected. It's like a backup plan to prevent you from the pain of defeat and weakening. For example, returning to the imaginary scene of you writing a book, what would happen if you realized the task was too complex for you? While you're struggling in front of your blank computer screen, you feel the dreadful possibility of failure and the weakening you would experience if you quit. Rather than face that possibility head on, your mind will come up with another, opposing, impulse. You might say to yourself: "I realize suddenly that I can't confine my creative genius to words. I shall devote myself to interpretive dance instead!" Or perhaps: "Writing is such vanity. True meaning comes from living life richly, so I shall plan a long vacation..." Sadly, people are often so afraid to let themselves want what they truly want that they repress it and turn away before they even start to follow it. They don't give their one true will a chance.

In reality, we all know what we really want. But we also believe we should prepare for compromise. Our other wills are secondary, weak alternatives that we don't even fully like. But without them, it would only be us and our one will standing against a cold and overpowering world. Indeed, it's hard to keep totally focused on what you truly want when you start to think about the pain involved in a possible defeat. So you end up teaching yourself not to want in order to avoid that potential future pain. With the secondary wills you try to ensure that you have an escape plan, a respectable flight. This is why so many people, like that 36-year-old woman, come to me (Shai), saying they don't know what they want, or else they tell me that they only want peace and quiet in their lives, which is probably the ultimate replacement-will.

I (Shai) encounter a common phenomenon in my therapeutic practice when I work with some single women who come to me seeking "spiritual transformation." In the process of our sessions, this spiritual desire reveals itself as an alternative will to what they really want: to marry and/or have children. Deep down, they are terrified of trying to find a man for fear of rejection, and they feel their single status as a social failure. Now they have created for themselves two wills, and they struggle to reconcile them. I've heard many such women attempt this reconciliation by telling me they hope their transformative inner work will "purify" and "ready" them so that the right man will want them without any struggle on their part. What happens if and when they manage to find the "right man"? They claim their thera-peutic work of transformation has ended successfully, and at once they shift their focus to the cultivation of their now-fulfilled original wish.

In professional contexts you can often find secondary wills emerging as executives struggle to attain success in their careers, striving to climb the corporate ladder while at the same time fantasizing about their retirement; the retirement dream is the alternative intended to cushion the pain of potential failure to reach the top. We laugh knowingly when politicians get caught in a scandal that ruins their careers, and they announce they are leaving office because they want "to spend more time with their family."

Another obstacle to connecting with one's original will is that it's usually more embarrassing than the replacement-wills. Our original wills are often more crude, a wish for some obvious external power. This makes them less respectable compared with replacement-wills that enhance our self-image. As a result we often prefer to hide away our original wills even from ourselves so we can say, "I don't know what I really want." We prefer to think there's a struggle going on between some "force" and our more sublime and selfless wills. This way we can appear as one torn by forces that pull in different directions. One can even feel like a martyr, tormented by the contradictions of one's soul. Just think of all the saints who described their own experience in exactly this way, as being torn between their sexual impulses and their divine urges. Remember, these are not external forces. These are your own wills: wills that don't match up with your self-image.

The heart of the problem is that your secondary wills and your original will start contradicting and competing with each other, so that you don't know what you wanted in the first place. Here's an example from my (Shai) therapy work, which you can analyze for yourself. When I posed the question: "What do you really want?" to a troubled forty-year-old psychologist, he revealed his multiple wishes: he wanted to be alone and to do things only with himself, *and* he wanted to experience a profound togetherness, connectivity, love and belonging. He wanted to become a leading figure, to be an influential front-of-the-stage person, *and* he longed to disappear from the limelight and lead a quiet and introverted life. He also wanted to earn a lot of money, *and* at the same time to lead a simple life in which the only thing that really mattered would be his inner values. It goes without saying that as a result of these conflicting wills this man felt completely paralyzed in his life. So what do you think was his true original will?

Yes, in reality he first wanted to be together and to belong, to lead others and to make a lot of money. But what if this grand plan would fail? In that case, he would want to disappear into a quiet, modest life. But in his mind, these wills appear together, as if he were two persons in one body.

What can we learn from this? *To be active and creative you need to have one major will at a time.* If you want several things at once it is unlikely you will attain any of them. This is true not only when the wills clearly contradict and cancel each other. Dispersed energy prevents fulfillment too. That's why it's essential to focus and concentrate all your energy on one central and declared will. Then direct that energy so that it flows completely in service to that will. All the secondary wills should function only as supporters and enhancers of the major will, and never as opponents.

I (Tim) always struggled with dividing my energy into too many directions, such as teaching, writing and publishing. Then a few years ago, after some deep reflection with my wife and business partner, we realized that all our activities had the common theme of transformation. Suddenly different pieces of my life started to fit together under this common purpose. This new awareness aligned my different wills so that they were no longer competing for my attention, but all started to fuse together as a seamless whole. It even became easier to say "no" to some activities that didn't fit. To my surprise, this has unlocked tremendous energy and renewed purpose. So if you have a cluster of wills that all feel original, and you can't let go of any of them, see if you can find a unifying theme that can become the one will to rule them all.

If you can maintain a unified state of will, you will find it extraordinarily potent and productive. In fact, now more than ever people need such a state. Why? We live in an unprecedented period in human history. For the first time our collective cultural systems do not directly control the individual's life. No one tells you how you should live and what meaning or purpose you should follow – at least not in most democracies. This creates a vacuum that you need to fill somehow with your own meaning and purpose. You're meant to create your life out of free will, but you receive very little by way of direction and training on how to do it, how to marshal and develop your inner resources. As a result, the very conditions that allow us to reach our unique and individual potential instead leave many people feeling a sense of inner powerlessness, alienation, apathy and dissatisfaction.

To create the inner resources you need to live a life with meaning, purpose and genuine free will, your first step is to gather all your dispersed energy into one will to rule them all. Here's what we suggest to make that happen in five consecutive stages.

1. *Work wisely to answer the question: "What do I really want?"* This is not just a beat-your-head-against-the-wall question. Used correctly it can serve as a stimulating force in your life. You will ask yourself this question to expose your many contradictory wills. Listen to whatever answers come up and, without filtering, write everything down. Then look at the list and search for your original will. To help you find it, ask: "If I had absolutely no fear of pain and disappointment, would I want this?"

I (Tim) stumbled upon a simple technique for revealing what you really want. To do this, you need a trusted friend – or even better, someone who is also doing the exercise. Find a secluded place like a park bench or a private room in your home. Give your partner your list of unfiltered wills you created from the paragraph above. Their job is to read those wills to you aloud one at a time, stating them in short, declarative sentences while looking straight into your eyes. For example, if you were Maria, then your partner would say:

"Maria wants to be a professional singer." (Pause)

"Maria wants to travel the world." (Pause)

"Maria wants to run her own small business." (Pause)

"Maria wants to devote her life to wildlife conservation." (Pause)

Your partner has to pause and watch carefully for your immediate physiological response to each statement. The amazing thing is, when your partner speaks your true will, you spontaneously smile. It's as if there is a joyful recognition of the truth that breaks forth from you. When a secondary will is mentioned, the response is often neutral – or sometimes even a scowl. It's actually a fun exercise. You can get even better results if your partner sometimes delivers statements that are the opposite of the ones on your list, so Maria's partner might say: "Maria wants a desk job at a big oil company." Don't ask one person more than five or six questions without a break. The effect wears down and you get muddy responses. This is why it is good for two people to do the exercise together, each asking the other 5–6 questions at a turn.

It's important to stress that what matters is recognizing your original will, not immediately following it. Some people might be afraid to admit their will because they think it's beyond their reach. While in some cases there are objective limitations (wanting to have a totally different body or wishing to have Einstein's mind) there's also a false sense of limitation that we put on ourselves. So examine carefully whether or not your wish belongs to the category of false limitations. To deal with this, write down anything that comes to mind that could get you closer to the fulfillment of your will. Then ask yourself if you are objectively capable of letting go of your replacement-wills and striving to make your original will happen.

After completing these steps, keep asking yourself the question, "What do I really want?" so that it becomes a constant refrain in your mind. Do this especially when you are making a choice about something. This will encourage the redirecting of your will-energy, refocusing it on your one central will.

2. *Get rid of your replacement-wills and the fear of weakening.* You can never determine whether you really want to follow your original will unless you get rid of your fake wills. Remember that these alternative wills are only made of anxiety and worry. As long as they attract some of your attention and energy, they will obstruct your vision and judgment. So recognize them for what they are. Tell yourself: "I don't really want this; this is only my fear in disguise." Next you'll need to free yourself from them completely. Do this by clearing away the fear of future failure. Be willing to endure the possible pain this may entail. Realize that this fear prevents you from truly being alive. If you feel the fear of pain is too overwhelming, consider enlisting the help of a therapist to overcome it.

3. *With this new clarity, determine if you want to follow your original will or to transform it.* Completing the first two stages, above, should give you an unobstructed state of mind. Now you are ready to evaluate your original will. Ask yourself: "Am I determined to follow through this will, even if its possible frustration or defeat might bring great disappointment?" There may be no immediately obvious answer, so give it some time to sink in. This process may lead you to conclude this original will is just not worth the trouble. In that case, you have to transform it. Use its raw passion to generate more inner power inside you. If you choose the path of true inner power, you'll find in Chapter Fourteen the guidelines you need for this kind of transformation.

4. *Choose the will that promises the greatest and most natural power.* If you're still not sure about your original will, take

a look again at the list of wills from stage one above. Examine the list this time as a selection of possible powers that you wish to attain. Then ask yourself: of all these possible expressions of power which one is both most empowering *and* relatively natural and effortless for me to obtain? The will you select must be realistic enough for you to fulfill. Realistic means more than just a lack of practical obstacles to attaining it. You must honestly feel strong passion and energy for it. It's not enough just to want. True ambition involves passion similar to the intensity of sexual desire – only far more continuous. So if your selected will doesn't arouse you, if this is only some lazy thought part of your primordial wish that likes fantasizing about having it all, effortlessly, then this is a will that will never come true.

5. *Stick to your selected will with all your might.* As soon as you've made your decision, do not waver. Stick to your will and don't let any alternative conflicting wills interfere with your single-minded intention. If your old fears and doubts return, clear them away. If your fears whisper that you've taken the wrong path, say to yourself: "It's better to make a passionate mistake than to want nothing forever." You can fully want only by sticking to two conditions. First: agree deeply to the danger of weakening; do not retreat if at first reality opposes your will. Second: vehemently reject your backup-wills. Remember they are products of a protective safety mechanism designed to catch you when you fall, but in fact they hold you back. Finally, when reality seems to oppose you, stay connected to your will even in times of great frustration. Resist the feeling of victimhood. This will help you keep the thread of desire strong within you, a filament of will that never breaks.

Will you find yourself saying…

"I want to work hard at my job and succeed. At the same time, I want to be a creative artist. I'll have to figure out which is my replacement-will, and then ask myself if my desire for what I really want is strong enough to go for it."

"I don't really want this current path that I'm on; it's a replacement-will – my fear in disguise."

"I am determined to follow through this one will I have chosen for myself. I want it with a passion as keen as sexual desire. I know I might get frustrated, might even be defeated. But I have the capacity to handle failure. I'm going to give it everything I've got."

Chapter Fourteen

Three secrets of true inner power

It's healthy to possess a feeling of inner power. It feels wonderful, as if you are on top of everything, and have become a master of your life.

When it comes to true power, however, this sense of mastery is not attained through exerting total control, nor by dominating everything by force of will. The awesome experience of inner power comes from knowing that life, just as it is, and no matter how bad it might get, cannot break the strong and solid self that you have built.

Possessing inner power is the unconscious longing of your psyche. Though unconscious, it's not that hard to uncover this longing. Just examine how you respond to moments of weakening or crisis. When you are losing power you feel your mind and body begin to break as if you are falling apart. So you react by quickly seeking to regain your sense of power and integration. For the ordinary mind this is achieved by relying on the false forms of inner power we have previously described: compensations, revenges, diversions, victim-feelings and replacement-wills. These forms are like bandages stuck on a wound – a wound that will never heal in this way.

That's why inner power provides a key to psychic health and balance. *You're healthy when you feel sufficiently powerful.* Whenever you settle into a deep feeling of inner power, it's like settling into the saddle of a strong horse, or into the driver's seat of a car with a powerful engine. You'll feel bigger than any obstacle or challenge you might meet. You'll know you can withstand the outer turbulence of life, and you'll feel powerful enough to overcome any inner resistance or frailty. This is why I (Shai) use the transformation of inner power to rehabilitate traumatized people who seem to have lost all sense of power. It effectively restores their psychic vitality.

How can you create this magnificent state of true power inside you? The secret lies in working correctly with your will-driven self.

When you experience a drive, urge, wish or ambition, where do you think this feeling comes from? You might say simply that it comes from your personality or ego. But this is not the original source. We declared at the beginning of this book that life is will, and so following this through logically, your individual will is just one expression of life's will that springs from the perpetual fountain of life's drive to emerge, become and expand.

So your will-driven self is not just a set of egoistical wishes. Your will is egoistical only the way that trees and bees and rivers and winds are egoistical – individual parts of a larger living whole. If you think of life as a holistic movement you can see that any individual's drive is in fact life's drive to overcome and outgrow itself. Natural evolution can be easily grasped in this way, rather than from the usual point of view of competing species and individuals. You can even understand the universe itself as a whole that ceaselessly moves to overcome and outgrow itself. Contemplate for a moment the immense leaps the universe has taken, from the superheated physical energy of the Big Bang to plasma-filled galaxies and stars, to stable chemical atoms and molecules which on earth (and perhaps countless other planets) grew into complex living forms. From physics to chemistry to biology, the universe overcomes and outgrows itself. In us, and perhaps many of our fellow creatures, the will of the universe has leapt the chasm from the biological to psychological dimension of consciousness. We *Homo sapiens* then reached further than our primate heritage, separating from the natural chain, reorganizing ourselves into massive communities and creating human culture, a virtual second driver of our own evolution. When you feel the surge of will inside you, you truly feel a spark of the totality of life's wish for expansion. It's a natural impulse that precedes psychology, a life force in you essentially no different than your sex drive.

Imagine yourself sitting outside at night under a brilliant starlit sky, and realize that the force that powers those stars is the exact same force that fuels your desires. Think of life in these terms and you'll soon fall in love with the gushing, rushing will inside of you. Connect the universe's great will to your individual will and you will find yourself throbbing with life in every cell. Spiritual doctrines that emphasize the feeling of oneness with life tend to miss this easy access point. You don't need to sit in a cave or climb to a mountaintop to get it: follow your will to its roots and at the bottom you'll find the ocean of life; your will its ecstatic wave. These spiritual doctrines make it even worse when they teach that you should let go of will and "want nothing" in order to connect with life. But that's not life; this is more like a frozen image of life. They say life is essentially emptiness. We say – with all the evidence of the living universe on our side – life is a restless passion for growth. Life always wants to become more of itself. *You* always want to become more of yourself. The urge to dance with life already burns within you. Release this urge and join the dance.

We humans are the manifestation of life's will. More than that, we are capable of becoming *aware* that this is our nature. This enables us to consciously decide what we wish to do with our will: whether we want to express it as it is, refine it or transform it. Most people respond to their will by simply striving to fulfill it. Sometimes they refine it because they realize that it's not socially acceptable. But their will is almost always directed to the external world of objects and people: they wish to appropriate external powers they find thrilling and overcome whatever stands in their way. This is, of course, far short of the full potential of life's will in you; it's limiting this great flame of passion in you to the narrow channel of instant gratification.

Life's will is neither good nor bad, but you definitely can use it for destructive or constructive ends. One of the most constructive directions you can take is turning part of life's will inwards. Instead of trying to become stronger in your external power struggles, direct life's will towards increasing your knowledge, intelligence, awareness and creativity. In this way life's will can urge you to transcend your current level of development.

When you direct your primordial wish "to have it all" inwards, the basic restlessness and dissatisfaction that drive you to want things in the world become a very positive kind of restlessness. It becomes an insatiable hunger for self-discovery and self-expansion. This transforms life's biological drive to become and expand into a spiritual drive for internal growth. Once you activate this internal power you'll realize there's much to overcome in your mind and psyche. Surprisingly, you will not feel distressed thinking of all the hard work that lies ahead. Instead you will be thrilled to break old limitations and begin re-creating yourself as a new type of human being. You will want to do it not because of some moral duty to become a "better person" but simply because you won't be able to accept old limitations: egoistical thoughts, infantile emotions, anxieties and apathy. You will want to be done with these because you will sense they are getting in the way of what is next for you.

What's great about self-overcoming is that you never feel it as an obligation or a chore. You will want to do it. Towards this purpose you are more than willing to abandon some of your external power, to forgo the habit of compensation, and to build an unbreakable self. This is what we call *volitional replacement*: choosing out of total freedom to let go of some of your powers, because through inner development you have outgrown them. In fact, volitional replacement is the only true form of development. You give up some powers for the same reason you throw away shoes that no longer fit your feet. So this is the flow of your transformation: turn life's will to expand inwards; realize that inside yourself, will becomes the passion for self-overcoming; use this passion to overcome your fragile self and produce true inner power.

"This may look good in theory," you may respond, "but how can it work in practice?" That's why the rest of this chapter as well as all of Chapter Fifteen consist of four major practices aimed to ground you in this process of transformation.

Practice 1: Use your competitive spirit. Competition is natural, inherent and constant in all living things: between individuals, between groups, and even between species. It's easy to grasp how this is so: Imagine you are one of several talented people who work individually in an office without any definite purpose, just "doing your job." Now imagine you have been told each worker has been assigned his or her own project and the one who does the best job of it will win a million dollar prize. Which scenario do you think will be more effective in making people fulfill their talents and work productively? Throughout human history bursts of innovation and advancement have come through competition. The play-writing contests of classical Athens produced great masterpieces still performed on stage 2,500 years later. The 1960s' "Space Race" between the USA and the USSR not only got humans to the moon, it produced advances that gave us much of the technology on which our modern life is based – including laptop computers and satellite TV. Our Capitalistic system works exactly in this way, utilizing the natural competitive spirit that throbs in human beings. While this system of course has serious drawbacks, our point is that competition gathers and focuses the individual's energies into the wish to win and to excel.

Do you have mixed feelings about competition? Many people do. Our culture is divided on the messages it sends. It encourages you to compete for your place in the world while at the same time telling you that you should be ashamed of your wish to reach for the top and leave everyone else behind. You're supposed to compete and supposed to conceal it. Especially for women in the workplace, these opposing messages are difficult to reconcile. Be too ambitious and assertive and others will call you "bitch." Be a team player, and wait your turn – and your turn may never come. So your first practice towards mastering the secrets of inner power is to acknowledge the competitive spirit that exists inside of you and to honor it. It's the way life has always moved forward, and it's the way for you to move forward, too. Give yourself permission to embrace this spirit – and be grateful that you live in a culture in which there are plenty of opportunities to compete, in sports, academics, business and even hobbies such as multi-player video games.

The question is not if it's right or wrong to compete. The question for you is: with *whom* do you choose to compete? On the path to true inner power the answer is clear: turn your competitive instinct into a competition against yourself. Engaging in power struggles with others is a lower form of competition. Winning in the higher form does not come at the expense of others. Winning when you compete with yourself means that you have overcome your lower, self-limiting impulses in favor of the stronger and freer you. One way to think of this is like athletes who compete for the sake of reaching their "personal best."

Think of your being as an arena of competition. The different forces inside you are different competitors. Ask yourself what internal forces you want to overcome. Laziness and fear – do you want to see them win or lose? What forces do you cheer for? What forces can make your whole being advance to the next stage? Map the field of your inner world in this way. Remember the competitors you choose to identify with will most probably win. There is a beautiful scene at the end of the French play *Cyrano de Bergerac* that epitomizes this competition between internal forces. Wounded and dying, Cyrano hallucinates an inner battle on the stage: "I know you now, old enemies of mine! Falsehood!" (he strikes the air with his sword)... "Compromise! Prejudice! Treachery! Surrender, I?" (he strikes). "No, never!"

Your lower competitive spirit often derives its energy from revenge-wishes, from wanting to prove yourself worthy and to overpower your enemies. Your higher competitive spirit, however, originates from your authentic being. You want to succeed and excel because you wish to draw all your potential towards becoming your best possible self. Instead of looking for external gratification, you seek a higher expression of yourself that surpasses whatever you have previously attained. The struggle that engages you isn't between you and your colleague or romantic partner or your father. It's between your present level of development and your next possible level. You advance in your life out of the wish to overcome the present limitations of your talents, creativity, insight and awareness. The higher competitive spirit in you drives you towards internal excellence. Your flaws and limitations don't scare you any more; they provide you with the energy you require to grow. They become raw materials, like the clay a sculptor uses to make a masterpiece, a masterpiece of wholeness and fulfillment.

Your envy can be enlisted towards this end; often considered a vice, envy can be harnessed as a positive force for transformation. Here's how to do it:

Make a list of all the things you envy other people for. Not only the people in your life; include role models that you admire. Think of anything and anyone who provokes the desire to compare your power with theirs. Then translate each envious comparison into something that you can do to overcome your own limitation. For example:

"His knowledge is far greater than mine," translates to:

> "What can I do to overcome my own limited knowledge?"
>
> "I envy her courage," translates to: "What can I do to overcome my fears and attain my next level of fearlessness?"

I (Tim) have three close friends whom I envy, and I do this practice regularly with them in mind. The first man is an award-winning writer. I envy his fame on the world stage. But I recognize that he's earned it through his passion and uncompromising dedication to his work. My envy becomes a spur to make my own writing better. The second is the leader of a global environmental organization. I envy his purpose and influence in moving the world away from destruction. This spurs me to think beyond my own life and become more engaged and committed towards global causes I believe in. The third is a doctor who has devoted his entire life to curing Alzheimer's disease. I envy his single-mindedness, which spurs me to become more focused and less scattered with my own energy. Where lower-level envy rejoices in others' downfall, higher-level envy rejoices in others' successes. The higher my friends go, the more they spur me on.

Practice 2: Turn any feeling into a source of power. By now you have already grasped that any feeling inside you, including negative feelings, is a will in disguise. This means everything within you is an expression of life's will, and so you have an abundance of power that you misinterpret as weakness. In this practice, similar to others you have learned earlier in this book, you can translate any feeling back into raw will, and then harness its power for your conscious purposes. For example:

I feel depressed, I want a different life translates to: "Something totally new wishes to come to life out of my innermost being."

I am so angry translates to: "I feel a surge of power that can move mountains."

I am frustrated translates to: "I am inspired to look for creative solutions that will lead me to a breakthrough."

I feel sexually suppressed translates to: "I'm like a dormant volcano of sexual desire; there's so much intensity in me that wants to be freely expressed."

Will is by nature an urgency to move forward, to grow in life, power and experience. So whenever a feeling is translated in you into a will, you're immediately back in the uninterrupted stream of life's great will. In this way you're no longer caught in the deluded thought that life is beyond your grasp. Remember, will is energy: it flows in you like a constant river. Following this metaphor, when you feel stuck in life, you are like a tiny river creature clinging to the weeds along the riverbank. You are actually expending a lot of energy to keep holding yourself in the same place. Let go of the weeds, which is what these practices help you do, and the river of life will move you immediately back into its flow. That river flows in you and it is you: an endless amount of energy.

Practice 3: Produce empowering feelings inside yourself without external stimuli. Any wish for external power is a wish to feel a power experience. When you picture yourself going on stage to collect your Nobel Prize while the entire world cheers and applauds, this fantasy is designed by your brain to provide you with a feeling of power. The stimulating image itself is not really what you seek; it's just a mediator between you and your longed-for power experience. The image is a symbol, in this case a symbol of the ultimate recognition and affirmation. It gives you a feeling of self-expansion, of being bigger than life. Here's the realization: *It is your mind that equates a particular object* (Nobel Prize) *as the symbol that grants you feelings of power* (affirmation and self-expansion). In reality, all these things and people are empty of any significance. They are like empty containers. Your mind chooses to pour into them the significance and meaning that you then desire. That's why some people consider BMWs or Porsches amazingly impressive objects: when they picture themselves behind the wheel they feel full of power, freedom and elegance, while others will think such fancy cars are a ridiculous waste of money. We all know the saying, "Beauty is in the eye of the beholder." We can adapt this as: *Meaning* (of a power-experience) *lies in the mind of the perceiver.*

When you deeply understand that the feelings you long for aren't dependent on the external power-experience, this means you can look for ways to find them through internal experience. The analogy that makes this clear is sexual fantasy. Your mind can produce extremely arousing physical reactions through vivid imagination alone. These fantasies can be so similar to the feelings occurring in an actual sexual encounter that some people get addicted to their fantasy life and fall into obsession. Of course, we're not suggesting that you should replay in your mind over and over the fantasy of winning the Nobel Prize in order to feel a power high! In fact, the problem with replaying a power fantasy is that it can entrap you in a state of waiting for the actual external thing to happen. Additionally, even when you have an actual external power experience, when it is over it tends to leave you with a sense of neurotic dissatisfaction: after you've received your Nobel Prize, you will feel even more craving for additional power experiences. In the language of addiction, this is known as the "law of diminishing returns," where more extreme experiences are required to get the same pleasurable feeling. The movie *The Wolf of Wall Street* depicts a fascinating real-life example of this, as Jordon Belfort and his company of scoundrel-traders engage in ever more risky behavior, screwing their clients and breaking the law to fuel the adrenaline rush of making more and more money – beyond anything they could possibly spend.

The solution to your longing to feel power experiences lies neither in fantasizing about them, nor in doing everything you can to get them. Instead you can learn to reach the feeling of the power experience directly through an inner process that isn't followed by the side effect of neurotic dissatisfaction, and does not lead to a path of addiction. In fact, the practice laid out for you here will instead give you increased energy for cultivating your inner power.

How do you reach this kind of power-experience? Start by imagining whatever power image you long for. Imagine this experience as vividly as a sexual fantasy until you can feel the desired power experience. Then simply strip the image away from the feeling. Feel those feelings directly by themselves, without the idea of the external experience in the way. The magic question that will help you connect with this feeling is: "What does it give me?" Use this question over and over again to gradually refine your crude desire for the external object until it feels very far away from you and unimportant. Then your inner space will be filled with the pure feeling of power, the feeling you were hoping to achieve all along.

Here's an example you can do as an exercise:

Let's say your wish is to be famous (if fame isn't something you want, try the exercise with whatever scenario you desire). Let this fantasy go wild for a moment. Visualize some intense situation in which your wish to become famous gets fulfilled in the most wonderful way imaginable. Perhaps you're surrounded by a group of admirers, or driving a limousine on your way to some major public appearance. What does this image give you? Suppose your answer is, "Endless power." Now ask

---

yourself, what does this endless power give you? Let's suppose your answer is, "A feeling that my life is meaningful." Now ask, "And what does this feeling that your life is meaningful give you?" Keep inquiring using this question until you hit the "bottom" of your mind. At the bottom of your mind the original object of desire (in this case fame) will seem to have vanished and become empty of meaning. You will see it as the empty container it really was. At the same time, you will actually be feeling more of what you really wanted – the real thing. The feeling of connection with what you really want will flood your internal domain and you will find yourself immersed in an ocean of pure power.

Try this practice now, before moving on to the next chapter, where you will learn the fourth transformational secret of inner power.

Will you find yourself saying…

"I so envy my friend. What's the quality s/he's got that I wish I was excellent at myself? Determination, of course. I can use my envy to spur me on in my inner competition to become my most determined self."

"I feel so frustrated and stuck right now. But I wonder what this feeling is telling me about my will? I think it translates as: 'Something totally new wishes to come to life out of my innermost being.' How can I use the powerful energy of this feeling to make change happen?"

"There goes my 'movie star' fantasy again! What does it give me? Unconditional admiration. What does that give me? Total acceptance. What does that give me?..." (And so on down to the bottom of your mind.)

Chapter Fifteen

Step down from the eternal seesaw

There is an ancient Taoist parable we both love that vividly captures the essence of true inner power:

A farmer had only one horse, and one day the horse ran away. The neighbors came by to console the farmer over his terrible loss. The farmer said, "What makes you think it is so terrible?"

A month later, the horse came home, bringing with her two beautiful wild horses. The neighbors became excited and rushed over to congratulate the farmer on his good fortune. The farmer said, "What makes you think this is good fortune?"

The farmer's son tried to ride one of the wild horses, but he was thrown and broke his leg. All the neighbors were very distressed. Such bad luck! The farmer said, "What makes you think this is bad luck?"

A war came, and every able-bodied man from the village was conscripted and sent into battle. Only the farmer's son with the broken leg was spared. The neighbors congratulated the farmer. "What makes you think this is so good?" said the farmer...

What makes this story such a perfect illustration of true inner power is the way the farmer treats both "good fortune" and "terrible losses" as equals. Now, many people do take this approach when it comes to their losses. As we pointed out in the chapter on compensation, when faced with a crisis, disease or dramatic failure, people often console themselves with the encouraging thought that no doubt this terrible thing will lead to something good just around the corner. As Little Orphan Annie sings, the sun will come out tomorrow! Or people think that there is some deeper meaning and purpose behind the bad event, some lesson perhaps. So they say, "Every cloud has a silver lining." They may even think that by having to endure this bad event they are somehow spared from something even worse. Then they say: "It was a blessing in disguise!" Indeed, we have so many clichés to help us deal with our times of weakness and loss. But if you are only using this approach to deal with your "bad" times, then you are using it only as a form of compensation.

The greatness of this Taoist story is that the farmer embraces this approach in "good" times and in "bad." Even when his power seems to rise, he rejects the temptation of satisfaction, which seems so odd to us at first. This endows his refusal to feel sad when bad things happen with exceptional depth and meaning. When your power declines and you don't collapse, *and* when your power increases and you don't rejoice, then you have left compensation behind. You have stepped down from the *eternal seesaw*.

The *eternal seesaw* is a metaphor that perfectly describes the alternating states of rising and falling in the world of power. At one moment you're high up, feeling giddy, looking down on your playmate on the other side of the board. Then, with a sudden lurch in your stomach, you drop to the bottom, while your friend shoots up above you. Of course in the playground your "downfalls" are not so distressing as you bounce up and down. They are even fun and playful. However, in real life you're usually swept away by the process of rising and falling. When your wishes are thwarted your whole being feels "down." Then when your wishes get fulfilled, your spirit is totally "uplifted." As we say more simply, "When you're up you're up, when you're down, you're down." This leaves you highly vulnerable and completely exposed to the seesaw's rapid and unpredictable fluctuations.

This happens not just in your occasional strong and significant experiences. It happens with every fleeting thought or brief impression. When an encouraging thought passes through your mind, you feel "good." When a distressing thought – some weakening memory or worry – arises, you feel "bad." The erratic ebb and flow of your thoughts and experiences as you ride up and down the seesaw gives rise to all your feelings. Experiences and thoughts of weakening evoke negative emotions in you. Anger, disappointment, fear, and sadness arise as attempts to resist, deny or push your moments of weakening away. Positive emotions, on the other hand, spring forth in a response to empowering experiences and thoughts; their existence also depends on this ever-changing movement of the seesaw.

We must admit this does have one bright spot: it creates exciting drama in your life. Like a never-ending soap opera, many moments of high emotion happen in every episode, with very few dull spots. But the price you pay for this is living in a constant state of existential tension. This tension is maintained so long as you believe, even subconsciously, that gaining power and avoiding weakness is what matters most in life. Like an addicted gambler, you then witness every moment as if it's a roll of the dice on which your fortune has been staked.

The path to true inner power offers you a different and less dramatic existence, yet one that leads to total freedom. You will cease to be vulnerable to the unpredictable increases and decreases of your power. Instead, you will learn to live in a *continuous state of power, a state that doesn't depend on moment-by-moment experiences of empowerment and weakening.* If you can attain this state even partially, it will significantly reduce your fear of weakening. This is the key to a life of inner power. When you are neither attached to empowering experiences nor afraid of weakening ones, that sets you free from the nauseating movement of the seesaw. You have the potential to live in a state beyond all "good" and "bad" experiences. This state, when fully achieved, doesn't tend to slacken or fade after the initial realization, as sometimes happens with spiritual illuminations. On the contrary, it actually deepens with time.

What is the secret to inner power? Step down from the eternal seesaw. Of course, as a participant in the world of power, you will always physically sit on the seesaw. Like the rest of us, you've got no choice. Life is this seesaw, and so at least externally and superficially you'll forever be exposed to the rising and falling of power. Nonetheless, internally you are definitely capable of stepping down. This will stop the feeling of the seesaw's agitating movements – that *giddiness* as you rise, and that *lurch* in the pit of your stomach as you fall.

Internally, you can stand outside this tireless game, and watch it as one total happening rather than as two opposing movements of "up" and "down."

When you stand on the seashore and watch the waves, you never think of them as two different phenomena, a trough and a crest, but as one inseparable dynamic – a wave. The low and the high points together create the surging force that crashes against the shore. If you could experience your own "lows" and "highs" with precisely the same detachment as the observer on the shore or the Taoist farmer, then you would be capable of transcending both suffering and happiness. Rudyard Kipling's famous poem "If" contains a few lines with exactly this insight:

> *If you can meet with Triumph and Disaster*
> *And treat these two imposters just the same...*

Most people want to attain happiness by putting an end to their suffering, so they devote much time and energy to seeking security and comfort. This is the same as only wanting empowering "good" experiences and avoiding weakening "bad" experiences. But on the eternal seesaw you can't avoid the up and down. True inner power offers a transcendent type of happiness that doesn't depend on whether you are up or down. In fact it's the only enduring happiness available to us in the world of power plays.

The question remains, how can you genuinely establish yourself in this transcendent point of view? The key may surprise you. True happiness emerges when you free yourself from your dependency on positive experiences of external power. As long as you're desperately attached to your external powers, you will fear the danger of your weakening. When the attachment falls away, the fear goes too. If you ever wish to take this leap, you need to overcome your tight grip on your own powers. Can you imagine in your greatest moments of elevation and success asking as calmly as the Taoist farmer: "What makes me think that this is good?"

The following practice is the most important and effective of all four practices in Chapters Fourteen and Fifteen that deal with true inner power. It offers the ultimate freedom, the final stepping down from the seesaw. We recommend you follow it daily for about three months. However, practicing it even for a few weeks should yield significant insights and experiences. We suggest you start by committing yourself for two weeks, and after that, to make the decision to persevere the full three months if you want to deeply internalize this state of freedom.

Get yourself a notebook and dedicate it wholly to this practice. Take it with you wherever you go. In this notebook divide each page into two columns. In the left column you will document all the empowering experiences, moments, or even fleeting thoughts that occur to you during one day. In the right column you will document all the weakening experiences, moments or even fleeting thoughts that occur to you during the day. The dichotomy must be very visual, presenting clearly one empowerment against one weakening. Only in this way will your eye and brain be able to capture the tireless

---

seesaw-like movements of your power. Imagine for example if you had an argument with your romantic partner. Afterwards, you might recall a cutting remark they said at the start of it that hurt your feelings. You would put that in the right column. You responded with a blunt recitation of your beloved's character flaws, and saw their suddenly pained expression. Put that in the left column. Eventually you apologized (right column) and then enjoyed the happy feelings of making up (left column).

Here is an example of how this documentation might look through the random experiences of a day:

Moments of empowerment	Moments of weakening
Looked at my bank account and found out that I'm doing really well	Woke up with a distressing thought about work
Thought about my upcoming vacation and found great comfort in it	Talked on the phone with my mother and was annoyed with her reluctance to accept my choices in life
Walked in nature and felt that all my problems vanished	Heard from my colleague that she is about to be promoted

Each evening dedicate fifteen minutes to contemplating everything you wrote in the two columns that day. After reading through one empowerment against one weakening, close your eyes and ask yourself: "What if these two columns, which seem like different kinds of experience, are in reality one total game, the movements of a single seesaw?" Then ask yourself: "Who am I outside this entire game?" As you contemplate this latter question, you are developing a growing sense of "you" as something separate from the game. This is crucial to establishing true inner power.

As you stick with this practice, each evening you will likely notice a feeling developing in you as if you are building a solid inner spine. That's the feeling of becoming a fully present and integrated being. This is your unbreakable self, the indestructible you.

This practice will become a new habit of mind. You will get used to considering the two seeming opposites as two complementary halves of the same phenomenon. It will become very hard for you to think of power as empowering and weakness as weakening. Both will be experienced like a single energy continuum that fluctuates, just as sunshine and rain are both part of the continuum of the weather. Power will become a totally different state, one that has nothing to do with gratifying experiences in your life. Power will be a state of freedom that is revealed when you go beyond this play of energy. Power will be your true self.

How will you experience this inner power? A thirty-year-old man who went through a long series of private sessions with me (Shai) described it well. He was a very introverted and gentle person, but after overcoming a traumatic memory from his high school days through applying my method, he could not restrain his excitement and bewilderment. "Now I realize," he said, "that in life one must feel powerful as an inner conviction, and not necessarily to be all the time on the side of the powerful in the play of life. It's strange: when I agree to be sometimes weak, this turns me into someone who has 'nothing to lose.'"

This feeling of power shares no similarity with the times in your life in which you grew in power or possessed some immense and special power. It's more of a rock-like state in which you feel neither high nor low. You simply feel whole and complete. When you look at the game of life from this state, it will seem as if the world of power no longer consists of endless struggles between opposing forces that rise and fall. Instead, the world will appear as one indivisible unit that doesn't really care if some parts of it are momentarily weakened and other parts enjoy a transitory peak. Great empires may come and go; this world of power remains forever unimpressed. In this way you will become one with the life that includes and embraces all of these elements. You will become the great consciousness that contains the game.

Will you find yourself saying, like the Taoist farmer...

"Thanks for congratulating me on my victory. Today, I just happen to be up on the eternal seesaw."

"What a crushing loss. Today, I just happen to be down on the eternal seesaw."

"My boss complimented me at work. At home my partner called me inconsiderate. So the eternal seesaw is working just fine. Now *who am I* outside this game?"

Chapter Sixteen

The ecstasy of compromise

Try this quick, two-part thought experiment:

First, imagine yourself demonstrating great power in the world. Pause and notice the scene your mind spontaneously created for you, including your inner sensations. For the second part of the experiment, visualize yourself demonstrating great power while in the middle of an intense quarrel with your partner or with a family member.

What were the images of the scene and inner sensations you selected? Most probably both of your images contained impressive outward actions and expressive feelings. In fact, it's very unlikely you would have visualized yourself behaving and emoting in a relaxed, soft, and flexible manner. Our minds automatically connect the idea of power with external acts. We also believe we have power when others perceive us as having it. Outward acts that cause others to react to us are the easiest to identify as powerful. And, since forceful or aggressive expressions of power cause others to react most strongly, we most easily turn to force and aggression when we think of demonstrating our power. Was this the case in your own thought experiment?

It's not so easy to separate the concept of power from our more familiar experiences of power-intoxication. When I (Shai) led a 7-month course on the topic of true inner power, after a few months one woman told me proudly how she had begun putting these teachings into practice in her daily life. One day her neighbors came to ask for her help. Determined to remain "authentic," she managed to "overcome" her tendency to feel uncomfortable with saying "no" by giving her neighbors a hefty shove, and slamming the door in their faces! If we return to the second image of our thought experiment – you in the midst of a quarrel – many people report that they feel powerful when they express themselves uninhibitedly. For example, when screaming at one's partner, many believe that they are finally expressing their "true self" and that they succeeded in fearlessly speaking their "truth"!

This thought might have passed through your mind while reading the chapters that dealt with true inner power: "Yes, I can accept that true inner power is the culmination of the whole process. But somewhere in the middle, before taking this leap, I need to learn to express myself fearlessly. I was a 'nice person' for too long, and I can't just shift at once to inner power while my external power hasn't been fulfilled yet. So first I want to free my wills and express them just as they are. I deserve this, even if it will hurt some people on the way."

However, forcefully expressing yourself is *not* a step forward on the path to true inner power. There's no intermediary stage in which your power and will "reawaken" and enjoy complete and reckless self-expression (to the horror of everyone around you) before maturing into inner power. That would be a grave misreading of this whole book, and a complete misunderstanding of your journey. In reality, free and uninhibited self-expression is a *regression*, not progress. Some spiritual communities actually practice being totally "honest" by telling everyone directly what they're feeling and thinking about them. But it seems a kind of fantasy, as if one was returning to a "natural" state before the influences of human culture. Calling something "natural" does not mean it is beneficial. As author Scott Peck wrote in *The Road Less Travelled*: "It is also natural to defecate in our pants and never brush our teeth."

True inner power doesn't pass through an intermediary "natural" stage in which you regress and shake off culture. Human culture, as expressed in you, is a great achievement, even in the mask you wear. It's not some oppressive force that pushes down your "authentic self." Your cultural self *is* the intermediary stage. It's a bridge between the raw aggression of your primordial wish and the emergence of your authentic self through the process of creating true inner power. Creating this kind of power can't be accomplished through self-expression. It requires inner transformation. This transformation can only take place on the solid ground of your cultural self. The analogy of the caterpillar and the butterfly might seem overused, but in this case it well illustrates our point: Imagine a caterpillar that strives to escape the cocoon (of culture), so that it can revert to its natural caterpillar state. That's regression. Transformation happens only in caterpillars wrapped in their cocoons, inwardly striving to grow wings and fly.

When it comes to true inner power, you need to start thinking of "power" as something other than expressions of force and aggression. To an observer, an expression of inner power might appear less powerful, or even lacking in power altogether. The reason for this is that inner power evokes almost no outside recognition from others, and rarely draws their appreciation. With inner power, you can be endlessly powerful, while others might consider you weak.

The main place for you to practice demonstrating your "invisible" inner power is in your intimate relationships with partners, children, parents, and friends. These close relationships are usually the first to get damaged by power struggles. You are not allowed to display your raw and unashamed willful self to the outside world, but in close relationships you often get to be more "authentic." In other words, you can struggle more explicitly for domination and control. The classic example of this is parents who are gracious and generous when company comes for dinner, but when alone with their own children they become sarcastic and abusive. When you're vying for dominion with the people you are close to, it's very hard to let yourself "lose." I (Tim) have found myself many times continuing to argue even after I've realized I was mistaken, because I just couldn't bare *being* wrong in front of this person. I vividly remember my grandmother arguing virulently with my father over the definition of a certain word until he furiously threw open his dictionary and shoved the definition in her face. I remember her face hardening as she read the lines. Then she spat back at him, "Well, that's *not* how the word is defined in *my* dictionary!"

The question for you is: would you agree to sometimes get weakened in the external battle of relationships in order to gain true power from within? This is a vital ingredient of transformation. It's important not to confuse this agreement with what happens in compensation. In compensation you replace your external loss with some internal gain. But compensation is a cheap trick. Its only job is to cover up the pain of your unavoidable external weakening. In transformation you *embrace the weakening*. The true power comes from the process of self-overcoming, winning the internal battle. So the apparent power loss – such as the perception of *being wrong* – doesn't bother you, and you don't need the fake power of compensation to make you feel better.

On the road to self-overcoming you will probably lose many external battles, since you will no longer invest your energy in standing on your toes and making sure your status will not be damaged. You will measure your achievement by a totally different scale of values. "What do others think of me?" won't matter much any more. Instead, these are the kinds of questions you'll ask: "How did I react?" "Am I putting the blame for my misery on the other or am I assuming full self-responsibility?" "Am I escaping my weakness by harboring revenge?" "Am I attacking and insulting just because I fear a humiliating moment of defeat?"

To demonstrate, let's use the example of an insult. Often when people get insulted, they either strike back to avenge their insult or withdraw and continue the fight in a secret inner dialogue, vanquishing the offender in the silence of their minds. But if your interest has shifted to gaining true inner power, a third possibility emerges. You can observe your own automatic response and then overcome it. Remember, inner power means defeating yourself: defeating that automatically-insulted self which cannot tolerate weakness and which must either lash out aggressively or respond with the all-too-familiar chain of compensation, revenge and concealment. When you are driven to attain a higher level of emotional and mental development, your aim becomes independence from such knee-jerk reactions. You don't allow your emotional state to be controlled by an insult hurled in your direction. You goal is a state in which you no longer fear insults and so you are free from the need to avenge it.

In the mesmerizing British drama *Starred Up*, a nineteen-year-old extremely violent prisoner attends a sort of anger-management prison group. One of the participants of the group insults the youth's mother. The young man jumps up, ready to attack the man who taunted him. The more trained prisoners dissuade him, guiding him instead to just sit there and take the insult quietly. "But I feel like a cunt!" the young man complains, while trying very hard to settle his breathing. "That's fine," responds the therapist of the group, "I feel every day like a cunt." Indeed, directing your energy towards observing your own reactions puts you in a weaker position. Externally it seems like the other has gained the upper hand. Yet in this beautiful example the other prisoners show the young delinquent that self-overcoming can be a new and better form of power.

The vast majority of people are far too invested in their habitual power-expressions to consider letting them go in times of struggle. People usually cling to their desire to win until they have no other choice, for example when their partner is on the doorstep threatening to leave for good. Only then do they give in. With true inner power, however, you let go of external power *especially* when you have a choice. You choose to replace external powers with internal powers, not out of a crisis of weakness but out of a deeper interest in inner power. Think of some of the leaders of the 20th century, many of them winners of the Nobel Peace Prize, who championed nonviolent resistance. While nonviolent resistance is not the same as inner power, the words of these men and women reveal that the principles of inner power were at work in them, enabling them to hold to their difficult path in the face of aggression and brutality:

Mahatma Gandhi: "Strength does not come from physical capacity. It comes from an indomitable will."

Martin Luther King, Jr.: "Nonviolence means avoiding not only external physical violence but also internal violence of spirit. You not only refuse to shoot a man, but you refuse to hate him."

Aung San Suu Kyi: "The only real prison is fear, and the only real freedom is freedom from fear."

While you have shifted your focus from outer to inner power, of course you know that others around you have not. They will most likely think you have become weaker and try to take advantage of this. That's one reason why some people feel reluctant to take the path of true inner power. The price seems too high, and the victory too quiet. Even after people get a genuine taste of true inner power, they tend to go back to their old habits such as rage, whining, and other forms of overt or covert domination. If these reactions seemed somewhat effective in the past, it's hard to imagine completely letting go of them. Only when you fully realize that screaming makes you look infantile, that defensiveness make you look ridiculous, that forcefulness only gives you fake power, can you really leave them all behind.

If you're really wishing for true power, for that amazing state of unbreakable self, you will want to wean yourself from your old reactions. These most often emerge when you come into conflict with someone. Here are four things you can do to break old habits and clear the way for your practice of inner power:

Pause: Before you pick up the phone to scream at someone, or fire off a crazed and angry e-mail or social media post, stop and take a few deep breaths. Contemplate what you are about to do. Ask yourself if this action will bear the sweet fruit of true power, or if it's just an outburst that will feel good for a moment, but will probably make things worse and possibly damage your relationship. Don't press "send" when angry; don't dial in distress.

Delay: Whenever you're in deep and blind rage, wait for three days before reacting. If you're seriously expected to answer sooner, just write: "Please let me respond in two or three days." The temptation will be strong to react at once, since your delay might imply the other is winning. Remind yourself that you are making this *choice* to delay, and that is actually true power.

Let go of any attempt to make the other see that you're right and he or she is wrong. The desire to see the other humbly admitting how brilliant you are and how blind they are is a childish fantasy. Experience your ability to let the fantasy go as a genuine inner victory.

Overcome your habitual resistance to weakening when it's time for you to apologize. You know *you're not destined to be someone who's never wrong*. Yet in the moment you don't want to admit your mistake. You get rigid. It takes willpower to overcome your stubborn self. Each time you apologize, it makes you stronger, more flexible and more capable of learning from your mistakes.

Does shifting to a path of inner power mean you should never aspire to express your powers in the visible world? Not at all. There *is* true external power, but its expression is an extension of your true inner power. The only thing that makes external power *false* power is your strong attachment to the powers of the world as if they were your only sources of power experience. It's the *dependency* that makes it false, not your participation in these power plays. True external power manifests as a direct result of your wish to overcome all internal limitations and to reach higher states of insight, wholeness and creativity. It's when your every action in the world is driven by the competition against yourself, never by comparisons with others. As the great baseball player Lou Gehrig once put it, "I love to win; but I love to lose almost as much. I love the thrill of victory, and I also love the challenge of defeat."

Since you don't look for your power in the world but derive it from inner sources, your active participation is more an expression and expansion of your self-overcoming. Because you're not power-obsessed, you'll only use non-forceful, harmonious methods to express your power, ambition and will. You'll never impose your power-fulfillments on a resisting world. If you want to glimpse this possibility, close your eyes for some time and ask yourself: "How could I fulfill what I want to achieve in non-forceful, harmonious ways? How could I faithfully follow my authentic wills, yet do it in a way that will blend beautifully in the world and in my relationships?"

In answer to this question, the most powerful principle is – compromise. That might seem kind of odd to you, perhaps even a letdown. After all, compromise is commonplace. Everybody makes compromises in their relationships. Yet often we do so with a sense of dissatisfaction. The problem is that people compromise grudgingly, with bitterness at not getting 100% of what they want. Very rarely do they compromise out of joy and profound respect. It is as if they have forgotten the meaning of the word itself. The Latin *compromissum* means "together" (*com-*) "promise" (-*promissum*). A compromise is a "together-promising" between two opposing wills that commits them to create something they both mutually want. With compromise, a single will becomes a joint will, and all the stronger for it. Seen from this perspective, compromise is actually the essence of relationships.

When you look deeply into the interconnection of all things, you see compromise woven into the very fabric of life. Nature is a complex system of many diverse wills, all valid and "right" in themselves just as your own will is perceived by you as valid and "right." This observation can set you on two very different paths. The first is fighting for your share, never pausing to legitimize others' wishes. The second is learning to appreciate the beauty and wisdom of compromise. A life of compromise without bitterness is an expression of true inner power: you have become powerful enough to give others the space to express themselves too.

True inner power helps you move into a new kind of relationship that includes the ability to compromise genuinely out of the full recognition of the other's existence. Most people are stuck on the lowest level of relationships where the other is not really a full and complete person. The other person is like a crude stick figure or a blurry hologram, a lifeless object that exists only as a projection of their wills and expectations. Their map of reality is not much different than a toddler's. To them, only one world exists – *mine!* Everyone else appears in their world only as potential fulfillers of their wishes. The psychological term for this is *Narcissism*, after the myth of the handsome youth who fell in love with his reflection. The word is often confused with vanity. But the real meaning is that for a narcissist, other people exist only as a reflection of themselves.

One place you see this in relationships is where a man puts a woman "up on a pedestal." His idealization seems like love, but the man has actually fallen in love with a projection of his subconscious archetypal image of the feminine (what Carl Jung called the *anima*). When the beloved woman acts differently than the man expects by expressing her own separate wishes or needs that don't fit his idea of who she is, he's shocked. It's like being rudely awoken from a nice dream. She's no longer "dreamy," existing as his idealization. She's stepped down from the pedestal. This is where a lot of fights begin in relationships, with each side struggling with all their might to reprogram the other side to keep to their proper role of one who behaves and responds just as their fantasy ideal would behave and respond. Of course women do this too – idealizing the man they love as a white knight or Prince Charming.

You start shifting to the second and higher level of relationships when you remind yourself that a relationship is a meeting between different worlds, and not something that takes place in *your* world. You're not the dictator of your relationship; there is someone else in it, and there's actually room for both of you. The relationship becomes an opportunity to participate in something greater than yourself. Often people romanticize intimate relationships by talking about "unity" and "egoless love," but the fact of the matter is that most of us haven't passed yet to the second level.

I (Tim) have been fortunate enough to have the experience of transitioning from the lower to the second level with my spouse, Teresa. There's no doubt about it, for the first few years of our relationship she had pretty much existed for me as a kind of projection. Even as I had grown to know her intimately, I had been in the relationship for what I got out of it. Then we started working together running training courses. I tried to be the dictator in our business, and it used to enrage me when she would criticize or suggest doing things a different way. Over time I realized she was picking up on things that I was missing in the classroom and in our client meetings. She proved right about a lot of things, and gradually I came to see that her perspective was like a second eye for our business. When I articulated this to her, Teresa was glad. She had patiently waited a long time for me to catch up with her.

Mature unity, a third level, happens only after you have fully acknowledged the otherness of the other. This is the realm of true love. Love is the expansion of our being that aspires to simultaneously see the other as a fully sovereign, appreciated, separate being, and at the same time to include him or her as an inseparable part of ourselves. To make that possible, you first need to expand your mind so that your attention no longer centers on your personal interest alone. Only through centerless attention can you see clearly that your "clashes" of wills are actually a refusal on your part to accommodate the will of the other. As long as you seek false external power, you will demand submission from the other. With your broadened mind, this demand seems meaningless and absurd. Gradually your desire to have your own way will slowly be replaced with the emerging desire for love, a love which embraces the will of the other as something as precious as your own. What you discover then is a tremendous increase in your joint energy – like the energy released in a fusion reaction when two atoms combine.

Try this practice whenever you enter into conflict with someone you love: look this person in the eye and recognize that this person exists *outside of you*, as a whole world of wills and wishes. You may note how rarely you recognize this fact. Imagine the person first as a blurry hologram then focus your attention on your beloved until he or she becomes three-dimensional, clearly defined as separate from you and real. Can you sense the person's fluidity, their variableness? See that they are not a certain fixed *way*, like some lifeless object. Instead perceive the person as a bundle of potentials and desires. Can you overcome your lower-level habits, and genuinely strive to recognize your beloved's otherness? Next, expand your awareness. Embrace the will of this person as a part of your world that gives you joy. Welcome the will of the other, and desire to see it flourish.

How does this shift in your awareness of the other in this exercise affect your automatic impulse to fight with him or her?

Will you find yourself saying…

"'What do others think of me?' – I remember when that question used to matter to me. Now the question that matters most is: 'How do I react to others?' Do I put the blame for my misery on them or am I assuming full self-responsibility?"

"How can I 'promise-together' with this person so that our combined wills can get more of what we want by working together than we could if we don't compromise?"

"I love you as an inseparable part of myself, and also as a person who exists outside myself as a separate world of wills and wishes of your very own. I welcome your will, and I desire to see it flourish."

Chapter Seventeen

Expanding your sense of presence

In this final chapter we will share a meditation practice to cultivate your true inner power and build your unbreakable self. Now, we anticipate that you recall that in Chapter One we pointed out that meditation designed to "still the mind" was difficult and seems an unnatural state. However, there are meditations that balance and relax the mind and body, and many people from a variety of traditions meditate as a discipline of mental clarity and self-mastery. For these techniques we have much respect. But what you will learn in this chapter is something entirely different from these other forms of meditation. The *expanded presence meditation* is the ground upon which your sense of inner power will flourish.

Do you ever have the feeling you are just one tiny, ephemeral dot in the vast space of the universe? Of course you do. We all do. It makes you feel quite fragile and vulnerable. But when you meditate to expand your sense of presence you get the opposite feeling. You experience yourself as a far bigger being, beyond the limitations of your familiar experience and the suffocating contraction of your daily thoughts and emotions. Your physical sensations also change. You no longer feel confined to dense matter. You feel extraordinarily spacious and boundless, as if all limitations have been shattered. The sense of immensity makes you feel far less susceptible to the threats of life's changing circumstances. It's the perfect antidote for feeling small and helpless. Through self-expansion all the power you've been looking to gain outside of yourself you now find as a source of ultimate power within.

It's important to note that expansion meditation is not some mystical or otherworldly experience – although mystics across many traditions have reported sensations of expanded presence and developed their own methods for attaining this state. One of the differences you will find with this practice is that it will come easily to you. I (Tim) have spent time living in Buddhist monasteries and diligently sitting for hours in meditation, and only a handful of times in 30 years have I reached anything close to this kind of state. Yet following Shai's method, I found this elusive presence simple to attain. With just a little practice you will find it as easy as riding a bicycle, only this ride will transform your mind and being.

The difference is that most schools of meditation set up a struggle between the primordial will and the will to meditate. One strives to "think of nothing" or "quiet the mind," or to hold the focus on the object of meditation or breathing, or to attain a state of "pure egoless non-attachment to thoughts." The primordial will resists entering states of nothingness or surrender or non-activity. Like a shark, it wants to keep restlessly moving through the waters of your mind. In the meditation you will soon experiment with, your primordial will and the goal of your meditation – maximum expansion – are aligned, not opposed. You are making the whole world "yours," and in the process gaining power. It fulfills your deepest desires. As a result, you experience total satisfaction.

We will now guide you through this meditation for the first time. If you already have a favorite form of meditation, you can use it to bring you into a state of awareness and presence; just make sure you go into it with clear intent and the context of true inner power in mind. This will change the direction of your practice. However, if you don't currently meditate, just follow the simple guidelines in these paragraphs. Most important, remember that your meditation is not meant to serve as some pain relief or momentary detachment from all your problems. Instead, use it as a ground for your everyday life, a ground from which you can freely and fearlessly embrace the world of power just as it is. The goal beyond this exercise is for you to establish this as a daily practice, as something you do at least four to five times per week.

Find a place to sit where you will be alone and undisturbed. If possible, choose a place where you can see a great distance – a balcony or a beach or a hillside. If you prefer to sit indoors or close your eyes, you can also do that. Begin with this clear intention: "Through this meditation I wish to form an unbreakable self which can withstand life's challenges and never flinch." Then start focusing on your sense of presence. You're always present, yet very rarely are you fully present. Most of the time only a small percentage of your being is truly there. Get in touch with your very sense of existence, with the awareness of your own being. We all say without thinking "I" or "I am" at the beginning of so many sentences. This means you're essentially aware of your presence, but you never make it your focus of attention.

The extraordinary thing about your presence is that it grows and spreads and expands the more you focus on it. Your focus is like its nourishment. The more you look, the greater it becomes until eventually it seems to be everywhere, not only filling your entire body and mind, but also the space that surrounds you and, in fact, the space that encompasses everything. As you focus on your presence, imagine it filling up your entire body from head to toe, like water poured into a cup. As soon as your body and mind are contained in this presence, allow it to spread outward to every point in space, as if the cup you have filled is now overflowing, filling everything. If you are indoors, let it break through the floor and walls and ceiling of the room

---

you're sitting it. If you are outdoors let it expand from the things near to you out to the horizon. Let it reach to the sky and to the core of the earth. Just breathe into it and let it expand, trying to reach its outermost limit, checking to see if there's a point in which it cannot expand anymore. Let it stretch to its maximum potential; as it expands, let it break all your known limitations and boundaries and fill the universe.

Hold your expanded presence for as long as it lasts naturally – about five minutes the first time, and then as you practice, for perhaps 10–15 minutes, longer if you wish. You will most probably find this a delightful state, a state of fullness and beauty and energy. When you are done, just sit still for a minute longer, to let the experience settle inside you.

Please try the exercise now, before you continue reading. At the end of the chapter you will get more guidance on how to continue and how to deal with potential obstacles you might face along the way.

As you meditate again and again, you will enhance and deepen this experience. Repeatedly entering into this state of unaffected, all-inclusive and ever expanding presence, you become like a tree driving its roots ever deeper into the ground so its branches can stretch ever higher towards the sky. As your presence becomes increasingly independent from life's precarious events and circumstances, it gradually eliminates all fears of your weakening. This provides you with a solid foundation for a total and fearless experience of life. Upon this foundation you can build your unbreakable self. Your meditation becomes your ultimate preparation for exposing yourself openly to the world of power.

I (Shai) use the expanded presence meditation specifically to help traumatized people regain their lost sense of power. Since we're all hurt by at least some degree of power loss, this insight is applicable to us all: When your mind and your whole being feel expanded, they also feel powerful enough to reclaim their lost power. In a way, it's all a matter of proportions: if you recall some drastic and painful event from your past, most chances are that you will remember yourself as being small and overpowered. This of course gives rise to a victim-consciousness, and leads to withdrawal into self-pity. But when the mind grows bigger through meditation, the influence the event has over you significantly diminishes. All at once there's no longer room for the "wretched victim" in your identity. The memory of the event no longer overpowers and overwhelms you. Instead the memory feels contained within the bigger context of your expanded mind, and that makes you capable of overcoming it at last.

The bliss and freedom that follow the expansion of your mind make the traumatizing event seem almost insignificant. Even the fact that you lost a lot of power in that singular moment does not seem to trouble you any more. In the context of your present expanded state it seems distant and not very important any more. That frees you completely from any need for the fake power of compensation to make you feel better. This sense of your greater presence arrives together with the clear signs of true inner power in your life: increased energy, vitality and positivity. In such a state there's no longer the feeling that your self needs mending. You no longer feel shattered nor damaged at all. This makes you capable of healing yourself, by correcting the sense of damaged self *from within* the wholeness and integration of the unbreakable self.

Many people try to heal their wounded memories while their mind and being are still contracted. But it is precisely this sense of smallness that made you so vulnerable during the trauma-tizing event. When you start feeling amazingly powerful, you're already halfway towards a complete healing. Imagine yourself as a small dot struggling to heal within the larger circle of the disturbing memory. Now picture that dot expanding into a great circle, so much bigger that the painful memory is now a small dot within it. As long as you are the small dot, therapy can only offer you sets of compensations, like "forgiveness" or "acceptance." However, when you're steeped in a profound state of maximum awareness, integration and presence from the expansion meditation, you cannot be intimidated by some fleeting memory. That's why you won't seek the protection and consolation of compensation.

Overcoming a tormenting memory is one possible use of your expanded sense of presence. More generally, when you reach an inner state of infinite being, you have gone beyond the external world of power. Since your expanded being possesses all the inner power you want, you don't need to desperately participate in external power plays, begging for power and evading weakness. In that way, the world shrinks while you become endless. When you're self-sufficient and self-nourishing in the deepest sense of these terms, you are free to engage, yet you don't *need* to.

Recall the description of the primordial wish from Chapter Three – this innate wish we all share to conquer the world and mold it to our desires. You can think of meditation as the act of turning that wish inward. When you turn the primordial wish inward, the ceaseless effort to control everything transforms into the urge to expand more and more. Essentially it's the same wish: to have our self spread throughout the entire cosmos. Just like Napoleon or Alexander the Great, who were driven to become omnipresent through conquest and triumph. But as you've learned, this primordial wish in its raw form is infantile and in constant conflict with reality. Yet attempts to condemn and suppress that will only create internal conflicts and suffering. Your primordial wish requires *transformation* for its final release.

This is the amazing outcome of expanded presence meditation: when the primordial wish is directed inwards, it can actually be fulfilled. In this way this utterly egoistical impulse can become a key to total liberation. As long as this wish is trapped in the search for power in the external world, it will strive for utter and uncompromising ownership through control and force. When it's released into your inner domain, your primordial will finds that it can spread unimpeded all over the universe. Its energy moves freely and blissfully to fulfill itself, and at the same time is able to relinquish its forceful struggle for control in the external world. You don't possess the world like a dictator; instead you fill it with your entire presence. Your presence, which initially was like a tiny seed, takes root and bursts forth, unfolding as the all-encompassing presence of all and everything.

In true inner power you turn the drive for endless power into the drive to transform. Transformation becomes your most preferred power. You're still a walking will, like everyone else, only now your impulses strive to change your being and consciousness. These are the same unconscious impulses that drove you to seek power in the world – more money, more sex, more status. But now they are like a wild river's rushing flow that has been diverted through channels for the sake of other uses – generating hydropower, irrigating crops, moderating floods. In this transformation you simply direct external urges internally, and they become energy you can use for whatever purposes you choose. This is similar to what you learned in Chapter Fourteen: how to divert the flow of the external compet-itive spirit into a competition of self-overcoming. It's a change of direction, not of essence.

When you get this principle, it becomes clear how meditation is a much better and much more effective expression of your primordial wish. It's as if this cosmic urge has become confused in human beings. In other life forms, the primordial will is rather straightforward: thrive, reproduce, evolve. But human consciousness is such a relatively new development on the planet, it seems as if the primordial will hardly knows how to express itself. Disoriented by the infinite possibilities of this new vessel (the mind), our primordial wish ends up wanting everything, forever – something that can never be gained in the external world.

When you look at giant corporations or at historical empires and conquerors, they all seem to be driven by the vision of themselves as possessors of the whole world. This insane fantasy can never be completely fulfilled, not even for the most powerful. It is inherent in the world of power that tensions, resistances, limitations, compromises and pressures constantly make everyone's power grow and recede. Even if you could take over the entire world, you would still want more and more, perhaps building spaceships to conquer the stars – think of the American impulse to plant a flag on the moon. When the primordial wish is directed outwards, its insatiable hunger is always frustrated (because it can never have enough), and is always fearful (because an unexpected force can arise to weaken it at any time). And so it can never rest. It must always be consuming, always be vigilant, becoming bloated and paranoid at the same time. Keep this bigger picture in mind as you begin your practice, and persevere.

Expansion meditation can be difficult at first, because of the lifelong habit of identifying our self with our thoughts and emotions. Still, meditation is far less difficult for you than conquering the world by force and struggle – which is what your unchecked primordial will would have you do. Remember, you have a better chance of overcoming your inner resistances and hindrances and becoming the master of the inner realm than you do of overcoming the world. When you set yourself on the path to inner power through meditative expansion, your primordial wish finally has a direction to move, unopposed by other wills.

Resistance comes only from your self, and victory by overcoming your self. As this happens it unleashes incredible energy for your transformation. Amazingly, you will discover such transformation redeems and fulfills your deepest unconscious wishes and yearnings:

- Your insistence that you hold the absolute truth of the world – knowing exactly how everything and everyone should be and what is "good" for the world – finds a new direction. You replace that image of the ideal world with the wish for an inner ideal world: attaining complete integrity, purity, and wholeness within yourself.
- Your hope to obtain absolute control of reality is transformed into the hope to become full owner of your inner life.
- Your dream of enthroning yourself the ruler of the world becomes a subtler experience of being one with all and everything, expanding more and more until you become so endless that you contain the world in your presence. This is the final fulfillment of the primordial wish – as a state of consciousness, and not as a megalomaniac ruler.

At first your new meditation practice will feel very freeing, relaxing and so enjoyable you will want to do it at least once a day. Our minds, however, naturally fall back into old patterns. It will take some willpower to follow through on this new practice, and we would like to leave you with some ideas to assist you.

If you have difficultly creating the initial sense of expansion: Start as before, sitting alone somewhere. Feel your sense of awareness, and fill it up inside yourself. Then notice other things around you, close by at first, then widening out. You want to move with this sense of widening and expanding your vision, and as you take in new things, keep the old ones in your field, so that you are taking in more and more. Include the dimension of sounds –

birds, waves, winds, traffic, music from a radio. Include smells and sensations – someone's cooking in the next apartment, a breeze on your face, the warmth of the sun. Push out to the horizon, the skyline, the sun and moon, the stars (the night sky can be an amazing experience this way).

Keep widening and expanding your presence, including everything – your own internal body sensations, your own feelings, thoughts and even the awareness that you are having this experience of expansion. Include other people, but not as they normally appear to you, with a constellation of ideas and emotions and judgments about this person and that person. You just let them appear in your world as one element of it.

Dealing with distractions: As you continue to expand your presence outwards, you may find your attention gets distracted. For example, a butterfly flits by. "Oh, how beautiful!" you inwardly exclaim. Then, if you pay attention, you will feel your mind starting to condense around it, attracted to this passing thing as if inwardly you are clinging to it. Thoughts about it will arise: "It's a monarch butterfly. I wonder if it is migrating to Mexico? It's getting cold out. If there's a frost this weekend, the thing could die. I read somewhere their numbers are diminishing with Climate Change. Should I build a butterfly garden in my back yard, plant some milkweed? I think that's what they eat..." Catch yourself in this form of mental attachment. It constricts your mind and moves you back into ordinary thinking and reacting to objects, rather than expanded presence. When this happens, let the object go. Release the butterfly in your mind by setting it back into the context of your expanded awareness. The key is to remember in this awareness you are to experience everything without attempting to change or influence anything external.

Turning the will's possessiveness to your advantage: One trick that can help you keep your will from condensing objects within your field of presence is to claim them as yours: *my* butterfly, *my* flower, *my* music, *my* airplane in the sky, *my* sun, *my* stars. This relaxes your will's urge to take over, and at the same time it shifts you ever deeper into a state of full presence, because by "my" you no longer mean "the thing I personally possess." Instead you mean, "the thing appearing in the world I am becoming one with." The word "my" becomes a powerful incantation of inclusion for your expanded presence.

Dealing with negative feelings towards objects: When you have begun to establish yourself in this meditation you can try something different with the powerful word "my." You can use it to better integrate objects in your field of presence that you have a negative reaction to. For example, if there's a wasp hovering nearby, instead of swatting at it and leaping away, say "my wasp" and let it be in the context of your presence. (Do keep in mind that there's nothing mystical going on here, you are inwardly becoming one with the world, not overpowering the world. So if you are sitting at an outdoor café and meditating and a bus swerves off the road in your direction, don't become one with the bus – get out of the way.)

Your presence is the greatest secret of your indestructible self. Activate it not only on a daily basis, but also whenever you feel you're hitting some insurmountable wall in your life, or a challenge that feels too big to overcome. At such times we often experience ourselves as small, as a tiny dot, and the wall or challenge as something too big to conquer. Use your presence meditation to make yourself so vast that the challenge becomes just a tiny dot within you. Similarly if you recall a harsh and painful memory, you probably feel small inside of it. Through your presence, invert this episode from your past until it becomes miniscule inside your vast being. Then you can begin to heal it, and let it go.

Will you find yourself saying…

"This challenge seems overwhelming right now. I feel tiny and helpless in the face of it, but that's okay. I can meditate with presence and become bigger than my problems. I'm unbreakable."

"I know I can't *control* reality, but through presence, I've got the amazing power to *become one* with it."

"Good morning world, you are utterly and completely *mine!*"

Epilogue

Is this the end of the journey? Have you arrived at a safe haven? Have we given you all the answers to all life's questions? Of course not! You now know the human mind was not made to be at peace. You are a walking will in a world of wills, a place of striving and strife. Your being evolved on this earth to flow within the creative, turbulent stream of life, forever active, awake and alive. As the philosopher Nietzsche once wrote:

Yes, I know whence I have sprung!
Insatiable as a flame I burn and consume myself!
Whatever I seize hold on becomes light, whatever I leave, ashes;
Certainly I am a flame.

You are life's flame. There is no final goal of development for you, no ultimate enlightenment, no state of perfect knowledge, no end point.

As a final word from the two of us: Beware ideas that give you comfort. When we encounter an idea that we like, one that helps us make sense of the world as a predictable, safe place, we tend to hold on to it. We make this idea into a Truth with a capital "T." In this way, ideas turn into beliefs. Beliefs only seem to be empowering. In fact, they weaken the mind. They become a mental straightjacket. We stop thinking, we stop adapting, we stop creating with our life, and instead seek to make reality conform to what we already know. So as your final practice, learn to examine your mind for comforting beliefs. Destroy old habits of thought and fixed clichés about how to live. Creatively overcome your own beliefs and rebuild your life, again and again, without an end.

You see, the indestructible you, your unbreakable self, is not a fortress for you to inhabit; it is a tool forged for your use in this continually creative process. As you keep developing your inner power with the practices in this book, you will find you have abundant, focused energy. Having signed Life's Contract, you will live boldly in the real world. You will not waste energy on replacements, compensations, revenge-wishes and concealments. You won't weaken yourself by identifying with the social mask you wear or the false subconscious of the victim. Your past traumas and outbursts of aggression won't hold you back either; instead you will transform those difficult experiences into fuel for your growth.

Stepping off the eternal seesaw, you will no longer be constrained by external measures of success and failure. You will witness both ups and downs as part of life's endless game. At the same time, you will grow in your ability to recognize the full personhood of others. This will allow you to love deeply and become adept at compromises. Becoming adept at aligning your will with the wills of others, you will learn to accomplish more together than you ever could alone. Finally, your ability to meditate with presence will daily nourish your primordial wish with a sense of expansion, deep satisfaction, and joy.

Yet even this will not be enough for you. Should you grasp all the ideas in this book at their deepest level and master all the practices with perfect fluidity, your restless mind would still be driven to overcome itself, expand beyond all you have learned, seek new vistas, discover new truths. This is exactly what we want for you. You are life's flame. Burn bright.

Definition of Key Terms

Will – The ceaseless drive to become more than one is. The drive to expand oneself through further experience, achievement and knowledge.

Power – The experience of will-fulfilment. The feeling that one has managed to take over a desired experience, achievement and knowledge.

Will precedes suffering – The principle that human suffering follows from frustration of the will. All negative emotions result from the frustration of one's wish to expand and grow in power.

Primordial wish – One's secret and mostly repressed yearning to control the world in order to attain fulfilment of all of one's wills.

The true self – The hidden self that lies behind our cultural mask and only wants to follow the will without shame or contradiction.

The false self – The social self that wears a self-image of a good and almost will-free person. Naturally, the great oppressor of the true self.

Primal narrative – The story we weave since childhood about the basic struggle between our true self and society. The most basic feeling we have about our position in the world of power struggles.

Replacement – The act of silent and embarrassing withdrawal from a field we failed to master, followed by the shift to another field which we more conveniently master.

Compensation – A sense of false inner power which we give to ourselves, whenever we fail to fulfil our will. Replacing a sense of failure with some empowering thought or emotion.

Revenge – Our attempt to correct our feeling of failure and weakness by getting even with those who weakened us (or with others who remind us of them).

Concealment – Our social pretense that we are good (almost will-free) and powerful (not really wounded by our experiences of weakening). The mask which covers up the deeper truth of our wills and their frustrations.

The true subconscious – The repressed world of our socially forbidden wills that is the real source of our emotions and actions.

The false subconscious – The story we weave about our source of agony and frustration. The story about ourselves as victims rather than ambitious beings.

Diversion – The manipulation we make to shift attention from our will-driven motivations to our story as helpless victims.

Trauma – The shock of powerlessness; experiences in which our will is almost completely crushed by others' momentary stronger wills.

Burst of aggression – Moments in life in which we fail to conceal our true self and primordial wish and do anything we can to achieve will-fulfilment. In such moments we are blind to the will-fulfilment of others.

True inner power – A state in which we are connected to a sense of self-expansion which does not depend on life's empowerments and weakenings.

The eternal seesaw – The consistent experience of ups and downs in life that makes us feel sometimes winners and sometimes losers.

Replacement wills – The alternative wills we prepare in case our original will would be rejected by life and society.

Volitional replacement – Choosing out of total freedom to let go of some of one's powers, because through inner development one has outgrown them.

Life's contract – An unwritten agreement we "sign" when we are born that we are willing to participate in the struggle of wills and the experience of weakness involved.

Inner competition – The transformation of the competitive spirit – comparing ourselves with others – into the effort to constantly transcend our own level of development. Overcoming ourselves instead of fighting others.

Compromise – The mature recognition that life is not meant to fully fulfil our own ambition but is actually a meeting place between different wills.

The expanded presence meditation – A meditation that focuses on the expansion of our sense of presence. Its purpose is to replace the power struggle with the world with an ever-growing sense of true inner power.

Bibliography

Wilson, Edward O. The Social Conquest of Earth. Liveright, 2012

Quote of Nassim Taleb taken from:
Uri Pasovski, an interview with Nassim Taleb, www.ynet.co.il,
23.5.2014

Quote of Malala Yousafzai taken from:
http://www.bbc.com/news/world-asia-23282662

Quotes of Near Death Experiences taken from:
http://www.near-death.com/experiences/research24.html#a04

Quote of Peter Belmi taken from:
Tali Shamir, an interview with Peter Belmi, www.ynet.co.il,
10.7.2014

Poem by Friedrich Nietzsche taken from:
Hollingdale, R.J. Nietzsche – The Man and His Philosophy.
Cambridge University Press, 1965

About the Authors

Shai Tubali is a thinker and an author who specializes in the field of self-transformation. His fourteen books in Hebrew (two of them have become best sellers; another received a prize from the Israeli Ministry of Education), six books in English and three books in German are all dedicated to establishing new pathways of genuine inner self-change. His book *The Seven Wisdoms of Life* was selected as a finalist in Foreword's IndieFab Book Of The Year Awards. For the past fourteen years he has been teaching spiritual transformation in Europe and Israel. He also teaches his "Expansion method" in international schools, workshops and private sessions. In his last book, *The Journey to Inner Power*, he first presented the principles of Power Psychology, which are also applied in *Indestructible You*.

Yearly international courses and trainings on Power Psychology and the Expansion Method are taught by Shai Tubali in Berlin, Germany, and are also broadcast online for far-distance learners. Learners can choose to be certified as guides of one or two of these methods. Online courses can be also obtained at any time. Shai Tubali and other certified guides are also available for private sessions either on Skype or in person. You can find more information at www.powerpsychology.org.

Tim Ward is an author, publisher and teacher. His passion in life is transformation. He has written eight books, most of them exploring philosophical and spiritual dimensions of life in different cultures and then relating them to our modern Western way of life. As publisher of Changemakers Books, Tim seeks to promote the works of other writers focused on personal and global transformation. Tim also co-owns Intermedia Communications Training, where he works as a communications expert advisor and teacher for international development and environment organizations worldwide. You can find out more about Tim's work at www.timwardsbooks.com and www.Inter mediaCommunicationsTraining.com.

Books by Shai Tubali

The Mystical Enlightenment of Friedrich Nietzsche
The Missing Revolution
The Seven Wisdoms of Life
The Journey to Inner Power
The White Light: A guide to bliss

Books by Tim Ward

What the Buddha Never Taught
The Great Dragon's Fleas
Arousing the Goddess: Sex and Love in the Buddhist Ruins
of India
Savage Breast: One Man's Search for the Goddess
Zombies on Kilimanjaro: A Father-Son Journey Above
the Clouds
The Author's Guide to Publishing and Marketing
(with John Hunt)
The Master Communicators Handbook (with Teresa Erickson)

The Journey to Inner Power

by Shai Tubali

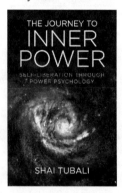

In this book, the ideas explored in *Indestructible You* are set forth in depth as a comprehensive exploration of Power Psychology – the psychological system created by Shai Tubali. The book is intended for therapists, psychologists, philosophers, academics, and others seeking a rich and full understanding of life and how to transform it:

If we could take the most intense and penetrating look into our psyche and strip away the layers, what would we find at our very core? Could we find the key to psychic health that unlocks our full creativity and potential? Working with hundreds of people around the world, therapist and author Shai Tubali came to realize that it was power that drove the human psyche: the primal urge for power, the loss of power, and the entangled and confused desires to regain power in our lives. Tubali created "psycho-transformative processes" to enable the men and women he worked with to uncover these hardest, hidden and most denied parts of the self, and then guided them to transform these parts into a source of true, revitalizing inner power.

The Journey to Inner Power sets the reader on this challenging new path to self-knowledge and self-liberation.

**CHANGE
MAKERS
BOOKS**

Changemakers publishes books for individuals committed to transforming their lives and transforming the world. Our readers seek to become positive, powerful agents of change. Changemakers books inform, inspire, and provide practical wisdom and skills to empower us to create the next chapter of humanity's future.

Please visit our website at www.changemakers-books.com